By Jon B.

Understanding Trauma Like a Millennial

Table of Contents

Chapter 1: Understanding Trauma - What It Is and How It Affects You

Trauma is an experience or event that overwhelms your ability to cope, leaving you feeling helpless, frightened, or powerless. There are many different forms of trauma, ranging from natural disasters, accidents, and physical injuries, to emotional, verbal, and sexual abuse, neglect, and violence. Trauma can also be the result of living in a war zone, experiencing a life-threatening illness, or witnessing a loved one die.

Knowing trauma as a deeply distressing or disturbing event that overwhelms an individual's ability to cope. Traumatic experiences can range from natural disasters and accidents to violence, abuse, and war. Trauma can have a profound impact on an individual's emotional, psychological, and physical well-being. Understanding what trauma is and how it affects you is an essential first step in healing and recovery.

What Is Trauma?

Trauma is a subjective experience that is defined by the individual's response to an event rather than the event itself. What may be traumatic for one person may not be traumatic for another. Trauma can be caused by a wide range of events, including natural disasters, accidents, physical or sexual abuse, violence, and war. Traumatic events can be sudden or prolonged, and they can occur at any stage of life.

Certain traumas can have a significant impact on an individual's physical, emotional, and psychological well-being. Some common symptoms of trauma include anxiety, depression, anger, irritability, hyperarousal, and avoidance. Trauma can also have a significant impact on an individual's relationships, work, and daily functioning.

How Trauma Affects You

Trauma is known to have a profound impact on certain individual's emotional, psychological, and physical well-being. Some of the ways in which trauma can affect you include:

1. Emotional impact: A trauma that can cause a range of emotional symptoms, including anxiety, fear, depression, anger, and guilt. This kind of trauma can also lead to feelings of shame and self-blame.

2. Psychological impact: Known traumas that can affect an individual's sense of self, leading to feelings of helplessness, hopelessness, and worthlessness. It can also affect an individual's beliefs about the world and others, leading to feelings of distrust and suspicion.

3. Physical impact: Tangible trauma can have a range of physical effects on the body, including sleep disturbances, fatigue, headaches, and chronic pain. Trauma can also lead to an increased risk of health problems such as heart disease, diabetes, and immune system dysfunction.

4. Social impact: Interacting trauma can affect an individual's relationships with others, leading to social isolation, mistrust, and difficulty forming and maintaining relationships.

Understanding the Impact of Trauma

It is important to understand the impact of trauma on your life in order to begin the process of healing and recovery. Some of the ways in which trauma can affect you include:

1. Intrusive thoughts and memories: Infiltrating trauma can cause intrusive thoughts and memories that can be difficult to manage. These thoughts and memories can be triggered by reminders of the traumatic event and can lead to feelings of anxiety and distress.

2. Avoidance: Distracting trauma can lead to avoidance behaviors, such as avoiding places or situations that remind you of the traumatic event. Avoidance behaviors can interfere with daily functioning and can make it difficult to engage in activities that you once enjoyed.

3. Hyperarousal: Increased tension can cause hyperarousal trauma , which is an increased state of arousal that can make it difficult to relax or concentrate. Hyperarousal can also lead to feelings of irritability, anger, and hypervigilance.

4. Dissociation: Distancing trauma can lead to dissociation, which is a disconnection between thoughts, feelings, and actions. Dissociation can make it difficult to remember details of the traumatic event and can lead to feelings of detachment and numbness.

5. Self-blame and shame: Unforgiving trauma can lead to feelings of self-blame and shame, which can prevent individuals from seeking help and support.

How to Heal from Trauma

Healing from trauma is a process that takes time, patience, and support. There are several steps that individuals can take to begin the process of healing from trauma, including:

1. Seek professional help:. It is important to seek professional help from a therapist or counselor who specializes in trauma. A trained professional can help you process your feelings, develop coping strategies, and work towards healing and recovery.

2. Practice self-care: Self-care is an important part of healing from trauma. This includes taking care of your physical, emotional, and psychological needs. Some self-care practices include getting enough sleep, eating a healthy diet, exercising regularly, and engaging in activities that you enjoy.

3. Connect with others: Certain social traumas can lead to social isolation, which can make it difficult to cope. It is important to connect with others who can offer support and understanding. This can include friends, family, or support groups.

4. Practice mindfulness: Mindfulness is a practice that involves being present in the moment and accepting your thoughts and feelings without judgment. Mindfulness can help you cope with difficult emotions and reduce stress and anxiety.

5. Take things one step at a time: Healing from trauma is a process that takes time. It is important to take things one step at a time and not expect to fully recover overnight. Be patient with yourself and celebrate small victories along the way.

Regardless of the cause, the experience of trauma can have a profound impact on your mental, physical, and emotional wellbeing. Trauma can change the way you think, feel, and act, and it can leave lasting scars that are difficult to heal. Understanding trauma, and its effects, is crucial to being able to recover from it.

Any type of trauma can have both immediate and long-term consequences. In the immediate aftermath of a traumatic event, you may experience shock, disbelief, and numbness. You may find it difficult to concentrate, sleep, or carry out daily tasks. You may have nightmares, flashbacks, or intrusive thoughts that make it hard to function. You may also experience physical symptoms such as headaches, nausea, or muscle tension.

Over time, if left untreated, trauma can lead to a wide range of mental and physical health problems. For example, you may develop post-traumatic stress disorder (PTSD), depression, anxiety, or substance abuse problems. You may experience chronic pain, heart disease, or other medical conditions that are associated with stress and trauma.

One of the most challenging aspects of trauma is that it can affect people differently. What might be traumatic for one person, may not be for another. This is because trauma is not just about the event itself, but about how you experience it. Your age, gender, personality, culture, and past experiences can all influence how you respond to trauma.

For example, children who experience trauma may have different reactions than adults. They may have trouble sleeping, wet the bed, or be clingy and anxious. They may also become angry, withdrawn, or have nightmares. Adolescents may react by engaging in risky behaviors such as substance abuse, or by becoming depressed and suicidal. Adults may have difficulty trusting others, may avoid certain situations, or may become irritable and aggressive.

Different traumas can also affect different parts of the brain and body, leading to a variety of symptoms. The amygdala, for example, is the part of the brain that processes fear and emotional memories. When trauma occurs, the amygdala can become overactive, leading to feelings of anxiety, panic, or hypervigilance. The prefrontal cortex, on the other hand, is responsible for regulating emotions and decision-making. Major traumas can impair the functioning of the prefrontal cortex, making it harder to manage emotions and make rational decisions.

Similarly, trauma can affect the body's stress response system, leading to an overactive fight-or-flight response. This can cause physical symptoms such as increased heart rate, sweating, and rapid breathing. Over time, chronic stress can lead to wear and tear on the body, increasing the risk of chronic illness and disease.

Despite the challenges of trauma, it is possible to recover and heal. Recovery involves a combination of strategies, including self-care, therapy, and support from others. Self-care involves taking care of your physical, emotional, and spiritual needs. This may involve exercise, healthy eating, relaxation techniques, and activities that bring you joy and pleasure.

Therapy can also be an important part of recovery. Different approaches to therapy may be helpful depending on the type of trauma you've experienced. Cognitive-behavioral therapy, for example, can help you change negative thought patterns and behaviors that are associated with trauma. Eye Movement Desensitization and Reprocessing (EMDR) therapy can help you process traumatic memories and reduce their emotional intensity. Other types of therapy, such as art therapy, music therapy, or mindfulness-based therapies, may also be helpful.

In addition to self-care and therapy, support from others is also crucial for recovery. This may include family, friends, support groups, or online communities. It is important to have people in your life who can listen to you, validate your experiences, and provide emotional support.

It is also important to recognize that recovery from trauma is a process, and it may take time. You may experience setbacks or feel like you are not making progress. It is important to be patient with yourself and to continue to seek help and support when you need it.

Lastly , trauma is a common experience that can have a significant impact on your mental, physical, and emotional wellbeing. It is important to understand what trauma is and how it affects you in order to be able to recover and heal. Recovery involves a combination of self-care, therapy, and support from others, and it may take time. With the right tools and support, however, it is possible to overcome the effects of trauma and to live a full and meaningful life. Trauma is a deeply distressing or disturbing event that can have a profound impact on an individual's emotional, psychological, and physical well-being. Understanding what trauma is and how it affects you is an essential first step in healing and recovery. Trauma can cause a range of emotional, psychological, physical, and social symptoms, including intrusive thoughts and memories, avoidance, hyperarousal, dissociation, and self-blame and shame. Healing from trauma is a process that takes time, patience, and support. Seeking professional help, practicing self-care, connecting with others, practicing mindfulness, and taking things one step at a time are all important steps in the healing process.

Notes:

Chapter 2: Coping Strategies for Trauma Survivors

Traumatic experiences can have a profound impact on your life, affecting the way you think, feel, and behave. Coping with trauma can be difficult, but it is essential to be able to move forward and heal. There are many coping strategies that trauma survivors can use to manage their symptoms and improve their quality of life.

One important coping strategy for trauma survivors is to practice self-care. Self-care involves taking care of your physical, emotional, and spiritual needs. This can include eating a healthy diet, getting enough sleep, exercising regularly, practicing relaxation techniques, and engaging in activities that bring you joy and pleasure.

In addition to self-care, therapy can be a helpful coping strategy for trauma survivors. Different types of therapy may be beneficial depending on the type of trauma you've experienced. Cognitive-behavioral therapy, for example, can help you change negative thought patterns and behaviors that are associated with trauma. Eye Movement Desensitization and Reprocessing (EMDR) therapy can help you process traumatic memories and reduce their emotional intensity. Other types of therapy, such as art therapy, music therapy, or mindfulness-based therapies, may also be helpful.

Another important coping strategy for trauma survivors is to practice mindfulness. Mindfulness involves paying attention to the present moment without judgment. It can help you become more aware of your thoughts, feelings, and physical sensations, and can help you manage stress and anxiety. Mindfulness techniques can include meditation, deep breathing, and progressive muscle relaxation.

Support from others is also crucial for coping with trauma. This may include family, friends, support groups, or online communities. It is important to have people in your life who can listen to you, validate your experiences, and provide emotional support.

Trauma survivors can also benefit from learning coping skills that can help them manage their emotions and behaviors. Coping skills can include techniques such as grounding, visualization, and assertiveness training. Grounding techniques involve focusing on your senses and surroundings to help you stay present in the moment. Visualization techniques involve creating mental images that promote relaxation and calmness. Assertiveness training can help you learn how to communicate your needs and boundaries effectively.

For some trauma survivors, medication may also be a helpful coping strategy. Medication can help manage symptoms such as anxiety, depression, or sleep disturbances. It is important to work with a healthcare provider to determine if medication is right for you, and to monitor any potential side effects.

Finally, it is important for trauma survivors to develop a sense of meaning and purpose in their lives. This can involve setting goals and pursuing activities that are personally meaningful and fulfilling. It can also involve finding ways to give back to others, such as volunteering or engaging in advocacy work.

Different traumas can be challenging, but there are many coping strategies that can help trauma survivors manage their symptoms and improve their quality of life. Self-care, therapy, mindfulness, support from others, coping skills, medication, and finding meaning and purpose are all important strategies that can help trauma survivors heal and move forward. It is important to find the right combination of strategies that work for you, and to seek help and support when you need it. With the right tools and support, it is possible to overcome the effects of trauma and to live a full and meaningful life.

Strong traumas can have a profound impact on an individual's life, affecting their mental, emotional, and physical health. Trauma can result from a wide range of experiences, such as abuse, neglect, accidents, natural disasters, or acts of violence. The effects of trauma can be long-lasting and can significantly impair an individual's ability to function in their daily life. It is essential to understand the effects of trauma to help individuals cope with and overcome its impact.

The Effects of Trauma on the Brain

There are several ways that trauma can affect the brain. The amygdala, which is responsible for processing emotions such as fear and anxiety, can become hyperactive in response to trauma. This can lead to a heightened sense of fear and anxiety and can result in individuals feeling on edge or constantly on guard. The prefrontal cortex, which is responsible for decision-making, planning, and impulse control, can also be affected by trauma. Individuals who have experienced trauma may have difficulty making decisions, planning, and controlling their impulses, which can result in them engaging in risky or self-destructive behaviors.

Another part of the brain affected by trauma is the hippocampus, which is responsible for memory processing. The hippocampus can become damaged or shrink in response to trauma, which can result in memory problems or difficulty recalling traumatic events. This can lead to individuals feeling disconnected from their memories or feeling like they are reliving traumatic events.

The Effects of Trauma on Mental Health

Individuals who have experienced trauma are at a higher risk of developing mental health disorders such as post-traumatic stress disorder (PTSD), depression, anxiety, and substance abuse. PTSD is a common response to trauma and can involve symptoms such as flashbacks, nightmares, and intense feelings of anxiety or fear. Depression and anxiety can also be common responses to trauma and can involve symptoms such as low mood, feelings of hopelessness, and excessive worry or fear.

The Effects of Trauma on Physical Health

Trauma can also impact physical health. Individuals who have experienced trauma may be at a higher risk of developing chronic health conditions such as heart disease, diabetes, and autoimmune disorders. Trauma can also lead to physical symptoms such as chronic pain, headaches, and gastrointestinal problems. These physical symptoms can be challenging to manage and can significantly impact an individual's quality of life.

The Effects of Trauma on Relationships

Trauma can also impact relationships. Individuals who have experienced trauma may have difficulty trusting others or forming close relationships. They may also have difficulty with intimacy or may avoid intimacy altogether. Trauma can also impact the way individuals communicate and may result in them withdrawing or becoming aggressive in their interactions with others.

Coping with the Effects of Trauma

Coping with the effects of trauma can be challenging, but it is possible. Seeking professional help is essential in managing the effects of trauma. Therapies such as cognitive-behavioral therapy (CBT) and eye movement desensitization and reprocessing (EMDR) can be effective in treating trauma-related disorders such as PTSD.

Self-care is also an essential aspect of coping with the effects of trauma. Taking care of your physical, emotional, and spiritual needs can help you manage stress and improve your overall wellbeing. This can include eating a healthy diet, getting enough sleep, exercising regularly, practicing relaxation techniques, and engaging in activities that bring you joy and pleasure.

The Stress Response

When an individual experiences a traumatic event, the body's stress response is activated. This response is a natural and automatic reaction to danger, designed to help the body respond quickly to threats. The stress response is controlled by the sympathetic nervous system and involves the release of hormones such as adrenaline and cortisol. These hormones increase heart rate, blood pressure, and respiration, and prepare the body for action.

The Fight or Flight Response

The stress response triggers the fight or flight response, which is a survival mechanism designed to help individuals respond to immediate threats. The fight or flight response involves a range of physical changes that prepare the body for action, including increased heart rate, rapid breathing, and dilation of the pupils.

The Freeze Response

In some cases, the body may also enter a freeze response when faced with trauma. The freeze response is a survival mechanism that involves shutting down the body's normal responses to stress and danger. During the freeze response, the body may become immobile, and the individual may feel numb, disconnected, or dissociated from their surroundings.

The Long-Term Effects of Trauma on the Body

While the stress response and fight or flight response are designed to be short-term responses to immediate threats, repeated exposure to trauma can have long-term effects on the body. Prolonged exposure to stress and fear can cause physical changes in the body, including:

1. Increased inflammation: Trauma can cause the body to produce more inflammatory proteins, which can increase the risk of chronic health conditions such as heart disease, diabetes, and depression.

2. Changes in the immune system: Trauma can suppress the immune system, making individuals more vulnerable to infections and illnesses.

3. Chronic pain: Trauma can increase the risk of chronic pain conditions, such as fibromyalgia and chronic fatigue syndrome.

4. Digestive problems: Trauma can cause digestive problems such as irritable bowel syndrome (IBS) and other gastrointestinal disorders.

5. Sleep disturbances: Trauma can cause sleep disturbances such as insomnia, nightmares, and night terrors.

6. Changes in brain structure: Trauma can cause changes in brain structure, including a reduction in the size of the hippocampus, which is responsible for memory and learning.

Healing from Trauma

Healing from trauma involves addressing both the emotional and physical effects of trauma. While therapy and other forms of mental health support are essential for healing emotional and psychological trauma, addressing the physical effects of trauma is also important. Some strategies for healing the body after trauma include:

1. Exercise: Regular exercise can help reduce stress, improve sleep, and reduce inflammation.

2. Mind-body therapies: Mind-body therapies such as yoga, meditation, and tai chi can help reduce stress and promote relaxation.

3. Nutrition: Eating a healthy diet can help reduce inflammation and improve overall health.

4. Sleep hygiene: Developing good sleep habits, such as avoiding caffeine and screens before bedtime, can help improve sleep quality.

5. Acupuncture: Acupuncture may help reduce chronic pain and other physical symptoms of trauma.

Trauma can have a profound impact on the body, triggering the stress response and fight or flight response. Repeated exposure to trauma can lead to long-term physical changes in the body, including inflammation, changes in the immune system, chronic pain, digestive problems, sleep disturbances, and changes in brain structure. Healing from trauma involves addressing both the emotional and physical effects. Building social support is also crucial in coping with the effects of trauma. Having people in your life who can provide emotional support, validation, and practical assistance can help you cope with the effects of trauma. This can include family, friends, support groups, or online communities. It is essential to seek out support from others and to maintain social connections.

Notes:

Chapter 3: Building Resilience After Trauma

Building resilience after trauma can be a difficult task as it affects parts of the mind and body. However, it is possible to build resilience in the face of trauma and to overcome its effects. Resilience involves the ability to adapt and cope with stress and adversity, and it can be developed over time.

One important factor in building resilience after trauma is social support. Having people in your life who can provide emotional support, validation, and practical assistance can help you cope with the effects of trauma. This can include family, friends, support groups, or online communities. It is important to seek out support from others and to maintain social connections.

Another important factor in building resilience is self-care. Taking care of your physical, emotional, and spiritual needs can help you manage stress and improve your overall wellbeing. This can include eating a healthy diet, getting enough sleep, exercising regularly, practicing relaxation techniques, and engaging in activities that bring you joy and pleasure.

Cognitive-behavioral therapy can also be helpful in building resilience after trauma. This type of therapy can help you identify and change negative thought patterns and behaviors that are associated with trauma. It can also help you develop coping skills that can help you manage stress and anxiety.

Mindfulness practices can also be helpful in building resilience. Mindfulness involves paying attention to the present moment without judgment, and it can help you manage stress and anxiety. Mindfulness practices can include meditation, deep breathing, and progressive muscle relaxation.

Engaging in activities that promote positive emotions and positive relationships can also be helpful in building resilience. This can include hobbies, volunteering, and spending time with loved ones. These activities can help you build positive emotions and relationships that can provide a buffer against the effects of trauma.

Another important factor in building resilience is developing a sense of purpose and meaning in your life. This can involve setting goals and pursuing activities that are personally meaningful and fulfilling. It can also involve finding ways to give back to others, such as volunteering or engaging in advocacy work.

Finally, it is important to develop a positive mindset and to focus on your strengths and accomplishments. This can involve reframing negative thoughts and focusing on positive experiences and outcomes. It can also involve setting realistic goals and celebrating your progress and achievements.

Building resilience after trauma involves developing social support, practicing self-care, engaging in therapy, practicing mindfulness, engaging in positive activities, developing a sense of purpose and meaning, and developing a positive mindset. It is important to find the right combination of strategies that work for you and to seek help and support when you need it. With the right tools and support, it is possible to build resilience in the face of trauma and to overcome its effects.

Healing Trauma through Self-Compassion

Leaving a mark on an individual's life, while leaving emotional and physical scars that can be difficult to overcome is also trauma. Seeking professional help is important, developing self-compassion is also an essential aspect of healing from trauma. Self-compassion involves treating yourself with the same kindness, understanding, and compassion that you would offer to a good friend who is suffering. It is an essential component of healing from trauma, as it can help individuals navigate the emotional turmoil and distress that often accompany traumatic experiences. Trauma is a deeply distressing or disturbing experience that can have long-lasting effects on an individual's physical, emotional, and mental well-being. Most trauma can be caused by a range of experiences, including natural disasters, accidents, violence, or abuse. The effects of trauma can be far-reaching and can impact every aspect of an individual's life. However, there are steps individuals can take to promote healing and recovery after experiencing trauma.

One essential tool for healing after trauma is self-care. Self-care is any intentional activity an individual engages in to promote their physical, emotional, and mental well-being. Self-care practices can help individuals to manage stress, reduce symptoms of trauma, and promote healing of the mind, body, relationships, and spirit.

The Importance of Self-Compassion in Healing from Trauma

Self-compassion can be a powerful tool in healing from trauma. Traumatic experiences can leave individuals feeling isolated, alone, and overwhelmed. Developing self-compassion can help individuals move away from feelings of shame, self-blame, and self-criticism and towards a more accepting and kind relationship with themselves. Self-compassion can also help individuals develop a greater sense of emotional resilience and an ability to cope with difficult emotions, thoughts, and memories related to trauma.

Developing self-compassion is not always easy, especially for individuals who have experienced trauma. Traumatic experiences can result in individuals developing negative self-beliefs, feelings of shame, and self-blame. It can take time, patience, and practice to develop self-compassion.

One way to develop self-compassion is to practice self-kindness. This involves treating yourself with the same kindness and compassion that you would offer to a good friend who is suffering. This can involve talking to yourself in a gentle, supportive tone and engaging in activities that bring you joy and pleasure. For example, taking a relaxing bath, listening to music, or spending time in nature.

Another way to develop self-compassion is to practice mindfulness. Mindfulness involves being present in the moment and observing your thoughts and emotions without judgment. This can help individuals develop a greater sense of self-awareness and can help them move away from negative self-talk and self-blame.

Self-compassion can also involve reframing negative self-beliefs. Individuals who have experienced trauma may have developed negative self-beliefs, such as "I am worthless" or "I am to blame for what happened." Reframing these beliefs involves challenging negative self-talk and developing more positive self-beliefs. This can involve replacing negative self-talk with more positive affirmations, such as "I am worthy of love and compassion" or "I did the best I could given the circumstances."

Self-Compassion and Trauma Triggers

Trauma triggers are events or situations that can bring up memories, emotions, and physical sensations related to trauma. Developing self-compassion can be particularly helpful in managing trauma triggers. Self-compassion can help individuals become more aware of their triggers and can help them respond to triggers in a more self-compassionate and supportive way.

For example, if a trauma trigger occurs, instead of engaging in self-blame or self-criticism, individuals can practice self-compassion by acknowledging their feelings and offering themselves support and understanding. This can involve talking to themselves in a kind, supportive tone and engaging in self-care activities that help them feel calm and grounded.

The Benefits of Self-Compassion in Healing from Trauma

Developing self-compassion can have numerous benefits in healing from trauma. Some of these benefits include:

- Increased emotional resilience: Developing self-compassion can help individuals develop a greater sense of emotional resilience and an ability to cope with difficult emotions and situations.

- Increased self-awareness: Developing self-compassion can help individuals become more aware of their thoughts, feelings, and behaviors related to trauma.

- Improved relationships: Developing self-compassion can also help individuals develop more positive and supportive relationships with others, as they become more accepting and compassionate towards themselves.

- Reduced symptoms of anxiety and depression: Self-compassion has been found to be an effective tool in reducing symptoms of anxiety and depression, which are common in individuals who have experienced trauma.

- Improved physical health: Self-compassion has been found to have numerous physical health benefits, including reducing stress and inflammation, and improving immune function.

Self-Compassion Exercises

There are several exercises that individuals can practice to develop self-compassion. Some of these exercises include:

- Self-compassion meditation: This involves practicing mindfulness while directing loving-kindness and compassion towards oneself.

- Writing self-compassion letters: This involves writing a letter to oneself, offering compassion and understanding for a difficult experience.

- Self-compassion break: This involves taking a few minutes to acknowledge and validate difficult emotions and offer oneself compassion and support.

- Imagery exercise: This involves imagining a compassionate and nurturing figure offering love and support to oneself.

Self-compassion involves treating oneself with kindness, understanding, and compassion, and can help individuals navigate the emotional turmoil and distress that often accompany traumatic experiences. Developing self-compassion can take time, patience, and practice, but can have numerous benefits in healing from trauma, including increased emotional resilience, improved relationships, and reduced symptoms of anxiety and depression. Practicing self-compassion exercises, such as self-compassion meditation, writing self-compassion letters, and taking self-compassion breaks, can be helpful in developing self-compassion.

Self-Care: Healing the Mind and Body After Trauma

Trauma can have significant and long-lasting effects on an individual's mental and physical health. When traumatic experiences occur, the mind and body can become overwhelmed and find it challenging to cope with the aftermath. Trauma can take many forms, including physical, emotional, sexual, and psychological abuse, neglect, war, natural disasters, accidents, and other life-threatening events. In the aftermath of trauma, self-care can be an essential tool in helping individuals to recover and heal.

Self-care is the practice of engaging in activities and behaviors that promote physical and mental well-being. It is an intentional and proactive approach to taking care of oneself. After a traumatic experience, self-care becomes particularly critical. Engaging in self-care practices can help individuals to regain a sense of control, manage symptoms of trauma, and promote healing.

Physical self-care involves practices that promote physical health and well-being. Trauma can have significant physical effects, including chronic pain, fatigue, and changes in appetite and sleep patterns. Engaging in physical self-care practices can help individuals to manage these symptoms and promote physical healing.

One self-care practice for the body is regular exercise. Exercise has been shown to have numerous physical and mental health benefits, including reducing stress, improving mood, and promoting better sleep. Exercise can take many forms, including yoga, running, weightlifting, or dance. Finding a form of exercise that is enjoyable and fits into an individual's lifestyle can be an effective way to promote physical and mental health.

Another self-care practice for the body is getting enough sleep. Trauma can disrupt sleep patterns, leaving individuals feeling tired and fatigued. Getting enough sleep can help individuals to manage stress, reduce anxiety, and promote physical healing. Some strategies for promoting better sleep include establishing a consistent bedtime routine, avoiding caffeine and electronics before bedtime, and creating a comfortable sleep environment. Self-Care for the Body

The body's response to trauma can include physical symptoms such as headaches, muscle tension, and stomach problems. Self-care practices that promote physical health can be helpful in managing these symptoms and promoting healing.

One self-care practice for the body is exercise. Exercise is a powerful tool for reducing stress, improving mood, and promoting overall physical health. Engaging in regular exercise can help individuals to manage symptoms of trauma, such as anxiety and depression. Exercise can take many forms, including walking, running, swimming, and yoga.

Another self-care practice for the body is getting enough sleep. Trauma can disrupt sleep patterns, making it difficult to get a good night's rest. Getting enough sleep is essential for physical and mental health. It can help individuals to manage stress, improve memory and concentration, and promote overall well-being. To promote good sleep habits, individuals can establish a consistent sleep routine, avoid caffeine and alcohol before bedtime, and create a relaxing sleep environment.

Self-Care for the Mind

The mind is a complex and powerful part of the human body, and it can be profoundly affected by trauma. Trauma can impact an individual's thoughts, emotions, and behaviors, making it difficult to cope with everyday life. Self-care practices can help to restore balance to the mind and promote healing.

One of the most effective self-care practices for the mind is mindfulness. Mindfulness is the practice of paying attention to the present moment without judgment. It is a powerful tool for reducing stress, managing anxiety, and improving overall mental health. Mindfulness can take many forms, including meditation, breathing exercises, and yoga.

Another self-care practice for the mind is journaling. Journaling is a powerful tool for processing emotions and thoughts related to trauma. It can help individuals to explore their feelings and gain insight into their experiences. Writing can also be therapeutic, allowing individuals to express their emotions in a safe and private way.

Emotional self-care involves practices that promote emotional health and well-being. Trauma can have significant emotional effects, including anxiety, depression, and feelings of isolation and disconnection. Engaging in emotional self-care practices can help individuals to manage these symptoms and promote emotional healing.

One self-care practice for the emotions is mindfulness. Mindfulness is the practice of being present in the moment and focusing on one's thoughts, feelings, and sensations without judgment. Mindfulness can help individuals to manage stress, reduce anxiety, and promote emotional regulation. Mindfulness can take many forms, including meditation, breathing exercises, or simply taking time to focus on the present moment.

Another self-care practice for the emotions is journaling. Journaling is the practice of writing down one's thoughts and feelings. Journaling can help individuals to process their emotions, gain clarity, and promote emotional healing. Journaling can take many forms, including free writing, bullet journaling, or gratitude journaling.

Self-Care for Relationships

After a traumatic experience, individuals may struggle with feelings of isolation, fear, and mistrust. Self-care practices that promote healthy relationships can help individuals to connect with others and rebuild trust.

One self-care practice for relationships is seeking support from others. Trauma can be isolating, but it is essential to seek out support from trusted friends, family members, or mental health professionals. Talking about the experience can help individuals to process their emotions and gain perspective.

Another self-care practice for relationships is setting boundaries. After a traumatic experience, individuals may struggle with feelings of vulnerability and fear. Setting boundaries can help individuals to establish a sense of control and protect themselves from further harm. Boundaries can take many forms, including saying no to requests that feel overwhelming, limiting contact ,and social self-care involves practices that promote social connections and relationships. Trauma can leave individuals feeling isolated and disconnected from others, making social self-care practices particularly important for promoting healing and recovery.

One self-care practice for social connections is seeking support from others. Support can take many forms, including talking with friends or family members, joining a support group, or seeking out professional help. Seeking support can help individuals to feel less alone, process their emotions, and promote healing.

Another self-care practice for social connections is setting boundaries. Trauma can leave individuals feeling overwhelmed and exhausted, making it important to set boundaries to protect one's emotional and physical well-being. Setting boundaries can take many forms, including saying no to requests that feel overwhelming, limiting time spent on social media, or taking time away from work or other responsibilities.

the people who trigger anxiety, and establishing clear expectations with others.

Self-Care for Spirit

Trauma can shake an individual's beliefs, leaving them feeling lost, disconnected, and questioning their purpose. Self-care practices that promote spiritual health can help individuals to find meaning and purpose in life.

One self-care practice for the spirit is practicing gratitude. Gratitude is the practice of focusing on the positive aspects of life and being thankful for them. Gratitude can help individuals to shift their focus from negative experiences to positive ones and promote a sense of well-being. Practicing gratitude can take many forms, including keeping a gratitude journal, expressing gratitude to others, or taking time to appreciate the beauty of nature.

Another self-care practice for the spirit is engaging in activities that bring joy and meaning. Trauma can leave individuals feeling disconnected from things that once brought them joy. Engaging in activities that bring joy and meaning can help individuals to reconnect with their passions and promote a sense of purpose. Activities can take many forms, including hobbies, volunteer work, or spending time with loved ones. One self-care practice for the spirit is engaging in activities that promote a sense of connection to nature. Spending time in nature, whether it be going for a walk in the woods, gardening, or simply sitting outside and enjoying the natural world, can help individuals to feel more grounded and connected to the world around them. Connecting with nature can promote a sense of awe and wonder, which can be particularly healing after trauma.

Another self-care practice for the spirit is engaging in activities that promote a sense of connection to a higher power or spiritual practice. This may include prayer, meditation, or attending religious or spiritual services. Engaging in these activities can help individuals to find meaning and purpose, promote a sense of connection to something greater than themselves, and promote healing.

Self-Care as a Lifelong Practice

Self-care is not a one-time event but rather a lifelong practice. After a traumatic experience, self-care can be particularly critical in promoting healing and recovery. However, self-care is also an essential tool for maintaining overall well-being and preventing future trauma.

Self-care practices can take many forms, and it is essential to find practices that work best for individual needs and preferences. Engaging in self-care practices can help individuals to manage stress, reduce symptoms of trauma, and promote healing of the mind, body, relationships, and spirit.

It is important to note that self-care is not a substitute for professional mental health treatment. Trauma can have significant and long-lasting effects, and it is essential to seek out professional help if needed. Mental health professionals can provide specialized treatment and support for individuals dealing with trauma.

Self-care is an essential tool for promoting healing and recovery after trauma. Engaging in self-care practices can help individuals to regain a sense of control, manage symptoms of trauma, and promote healing of the mind, body, relationships, and spirit. Self-care practices can take many forms, including mindfulness, journaling, exercise, getting enough sleep, seeking support from others, setting boundaries, practicing gratitude, and engaging in activities that bring joy and meaning. It is important to find self-care practices that work best for individual needs and preferences. It is also essential to seek out professional help if needed, as self-care is not a substitute for professional mental health treatment.

Self-care is a lifelong practice that can promote overall well-being and prevent future trauma. Self-care is a vital tool for healing and recovery after trauma. Engaging in physical, emotional, social, and spiritual self-care practices can help individuals to manage symptoms of trauma, promote healing of the mind and body, and promote a sense of connection to something greater than themselves. It is important for individuals to find self-care practices that work for them and to incorporate them into their daily routines. With time and commitment, self-care can help individuals to move forward on their healing journey after experiencing

Chapter 4: Building Resilience After Trauma

Trauma can have a profound impact on an individual's life, leaving emotional and physical scars that can be difficult to overcome. However, many individuals are able to bounce back from trauma and develop resilience in the face of adversity. Resilience is the ability to adapt and cope in the face of stress, adversity, and trauma. Building resilience is an important aspect of healing from trauma and can help individuals develop the skills and resources they need to navigate difficult situations.

Resilience is the ability to adapt and recover from adversity. Building resilience after trauma involves developing a set of skills and strategies that can help individuals to manage stress, cope with difficult emotions, and promote healing of the mind and body.

Emotional Regulation

Emotional regulation is the ability to manage one's emotions in a healthy and adaptive way. After experiencing trauma, individuals may feel overwhelmed by difficult emotions such as anxiety, anger, and sadness. Learning to regulate these emotions can help individuals to manage stress and promote healing.

One strategy for emotional regulation is practicing mindfulness. Mindfulness involves focusing on the present moment without judgment. Engaging in mindfulness practices, such as meditation or deep breathing exercises, can help individuals to manage difficult emotions and promote a sense of calm and relaxation.

Another strategy for emotional regulation is identifying and challenging negative thoughts. Trauma can lead to negative thinking patterns, such as self-blame or feelings of hopelessness. Learning to recognize these patterns and challenge them can help individuals to shift their thinking and promote more positive emotions.

Social Support

Social support is a critical component of building resilience after trauma. Connecting with others who have experienced trauma or who are supportive can provide a sense of belonging and validation, as well as practical assistance when needed.

One strategy for building social support is joining a support group. Support groups provide a safe space for individuals to share their experiences, connect with others, and receive emotional support. Support groups can also provide practical information and resources for managing the effects of trauma.

Another strategy for building social support is reaching out to friends and family members. Talking with loved ones can provide a sense of connection and validation, as well as practical assistance when needed. It is important for individuals to identify people in their lives who are supportive and can provide a listening ear.

Self-Care

Self-care is another important strategy for building resilience after trauma. Engaging in self-care practices can help individuals to manage stress, promote healing, and foster a sense of well-being.

One strategy for self-care is engaging in physical activity. Exercise has been shown to have numerous physical and mental health benefits, including reducing stress, improving mood, and promoting better sleep. Finding a form of exercise that is enjoyable and fits into an individual's lifestyle can be an effective way to promote physical and mental health.

Another strategy for self-care is engaging in activities that bring pleasure and joy. Trauma can leave individuals feeling disconnected and unhappy. Engaging in activities that bring joy, such as listening to music, reading, or spending time with friends, can help individuals to reconnect with positive emotions and promote healing.

Cognitive Restructuring

Cognitive restructuring involves changing negative thought patterns and beliefs. After experiencing trauma, individuals may develop negative beliefs about themselves, the world, and their future. Cognitive restructuring involves challenging these beliefs and developing more positive and adaptive ways of thinking.

One strategy for cognitive restructuring is reframing negative thoughts. Reframing involves looking at a situation in a more positive light. For example, instead of thinking "I can't do this," an individual might reframe the thought to "This is difficult, but I can handle it."

Another strategy for cognitive restructuring is using positive affirmations. Affirmations are positive statements that can help individuals to shift their thinking and promote more positive emotions. Examples of affirmations might include "I am strong," or "I am worthy of love and respect."

Gratitude

Gratitude is the practice of focusing on the positive aspects of life and expressing appreciation for them. Cultivating a sense of gratitude can promote positive emotions and help individuals to build resilience after trauma.

One strategy for practicing gratitude is keeping a gratitude journal. Writing down three things that an individual is grateful for each day can help to shift their focus to positive aspects of their life and promote feelings of well-being.

Another strategy for practicing gratitude is expressing appreciation to others. Taking time to thank friends, family members, or colleagues for their support and assistance can help individuals to feel more connected and promote positive emotions.

Positive Coping Strategies

Positive coping strategies involve engaging in healthy and adaptive behaviors to manage stress and promote healing. After experiencing trauma, individuals may turn to unhealthy coping strategies, such as substance abuse or self-harm, to manage difficult emotions. Learning and practicing positive coping strategies can help individuals to manage stress in a healthy and adaptive way.

One strategy for positive coping is relaxation techniques. Engaging in relaxation techniques, such as progressive muscle relaxation or guided imagery, can help individuals to manage stress and promote a sense of calm and relaxation.

Another strategy for positive coping is engaging in activities that promote self-expression. Engaging in creative activities, such as writing, drawing, or dancing, can help individuals to express difficult emotions in a healthy and adaptive way.

Factors That Contribute to Resilience

Resilience is influenced by a variety of factors, including:

- Social support: Having a strong network of supportive relationships can help individuals cope with stress and adversity.

- Positive coping strategies: Using healthy coping strategies, such as mindfulness, exercise, and journaling, can help individuals manage stress and build resilience.

- Positive self-image: Having a positive self-image and sense of self-worth can help individuals navigate difficult situations.

- Flexibility: Being able to adapt to changing circumstances and situations is an important aspect of resilience.

- Sense of purpose: Having a sense of purpose and meaning in life can help individuals navigate difficult situations and find hope and meaning in their experiences.

- Problem-solving skills: Developing problem-solving skills can help individuals identify solutions and navigate difficult situations.

Building Resilience

There are several steps individuals can take to build resilience after experiencing trauma. These include:

1. Developing a strong support network: Building strong relationships with family, friends, and community members can provide individuals with emotional support and help them navigate difficult situations.

2. Practicing self-care: Engaging in healthy self-care practices, such as regular exercise, healthy eating, and stress reduction techniques, can help individuals build resilience.

3. Finding meaning in the experience: While trauma can be incredibly painful, it can also provide individuals with an opportunity to find meaning and purpose in their experiences. Engaging in activities that bring meaning and purpose can help individuals build resilience and find hope in difficult situations.

4. Using positive coping strategies: Using healthy coping strategies, such as mindfulness, meditation, and journaling, can help individuals manage stress and build resilience.

5. Developing problem-solving skills: Learning how to identify problems and find solutions can help individuals navigate difficult situations and build resilience.

6. Cultivating a positive self-image: Developing a positive self-image and sense of self-worth can help individuals build resilience and navigate difficult situations.

Building resilience after trauma is an important aspect of healing and recovery. Resilience is the ability to adapt and cope in the face of stress, adversity, and trauma, and can be developed through a variety of factors, including social support, positive coping strategies, positive self-image, flexibility, sense of purpose, and problem-solving skills. Building resilience involves developing a strong support network, practicing self-care, finding meaning in the experience, using positive coping strategies, developing problem-solving skills, and cultivating a positive self-image. While building resilience takes time, patience, and practice, it can have numerous benefits in healing from trauma, including increased emotional resilience, improved relationships, and a greater sense of purpose and meaning in life.

Notes:

Chapter 5: Building a Support System: Identifying and Nurturing Your Support Network

Building and maintaining a strong support system is crucial for anyone, but especially for individuals who have experienced trauma. A support network can provide emotional support, practical help, and a sense of belonging, which can all aid in healing and recovery. In this chapter, we will explore the importance of having a support system and provide tips for identifying and nurturing your own support network.

Why a Support System is Important:

Trauma can have a significant impact on an individual's life, and the journey to healing and recovery can be challenging. A support system can provide a sense of safety and security during this process. It can also help individuals cope with the emotional and physical effects of trauma and provide practical assistance when needed.

Support systems can also help individuals build resilience and develop a more positive outlook on life. When individuals feel supported and connected to others, they may be more likely to engage in activities that promote well-being and take steps towards a more fulfilling life.

Identifying Your Support Network:

Identifying and building a support network can be challenging, especially for individuals who may have experienced relational trauma or who struggle with trust issues. However, it is important to recognize that support can come from a variety of sources and does not necessarily have to be limited to close family or friends.

Some potential sources of support include:

Identifying a support network is only the first step. It is important to nurture these relationships and maintain open communication to ensure that the support is ongoing.

Some tips for nurturing your support network include:

1. Communicate your needs: It is important to communicate your needs and expectations clearly to those in your support network. Let them know how they can help and what kind of support you need.

2. Practice active listening: Listen actively and empathetically when others in your support network share their experiences or concerns.

3. Offer support to others: Building a support system is a two-way street. Offer support and encouragement to others in your network, and be willing to provide practical assistance when needed.

4. Set boundaries: It is important to set boundaries and communicate them clearly with those in your support network. This can help prevent feelings of overwhelm or burnout.

5. Celebrate successes: Celebrate successes and milestones with those in your support network. This can help build a sense of connection and positivity.

Building and maintaining a support network is crucial for individuals who have experienced trauma. A support system can provide emotional support, practical help, and a sense of belonging, which can all aid in healing and recovery. Identifying and building a support network can be challenging, but it is important to recognize that support can come from a variety of sources. Nurturing these relationships and maintaining open communication is essential to ensure that the support is ongoing.

The aftermath of trauma can be a lonely and isolating experience, which is why it's important to have a support system in place. A support network can provide emotional support, practical help, and a sense of belonging, which are all essential elements in the healing and recovery process. This chapter will explore the importance of having a support system, identify potential sources of support, and provide tips on how to nurture those relationships.

The Importance of a Support System:

Trauma can have a significant impact on an individual's life, affecting their physical and emotional well-being, relationships, and overall quality of life. A support system can provide a sense of safety and security, which is crucial for individuals who are struggling with the aftermath of trauma.

Support systems can offer emotional support, which can help individuals process their experiences and emotions, reduce feelings of isolation and loneliness, and promote a sense of belonging. Having someone to talk to and confide in can help individuals feel less overwhelmed and provide a sense of validation that their experiences and emotions are real and valid.

Practical support, such as help with transportation, meals, or childcare, can also be essential in the aftermath of trauma. This type of support can help individuals focus on their healing and recovery by removing barriers and distractions that can hinder the process.

Sources of Support:

A support system can come from a variety of sources, and it's important to recognize that support doesn't necessarily have to come from close friends or family members. Some potential sources of support include:

1. Family and Friends: Family and friends are often the first source of support that comes to mind. These relationships can provide a sense of familiarity and comfort, and can be a source of emotional and practical support.

   However, it's important to recognize that not all family and friends may be able to provide the support that an individual needs, and in some cases, they may be the source of trauma. It's essential to identify those individuals in your life who are supportive and trustworthy, and build strong relationships with them.

2. Therapists and Support Groups: Mental health professionals and support groups can provide a safe and supportive environment for individuals to share their experiences and connect with others who have gone through similar experiences.

   Therapists can offer emotional support, guidance, and a safe space to process and work through emotions and experiences. Support groups can offer peer support, validation, and the opportunity to connect with others who understand what you're going through.

3. Faith Communities: For individuals who are religious, faith communities can provide a sense of belonging and support. Many religious communities have support groups and outreach programs for individuals who have experienced trauma.

   Faith communities can provide a sense of community and a shared sense of purpose that can be a source of comfort and support. However, it's important to recognize that not all individuals may feel comfortable or supported by their faith community, and it's important to find the right fit.

4. Online Communities: Online communities can provide a sense of connection and support for individuals who may be geographically isolated or have difficulty connecting with others in person. Many online forums and support groups are available for individuals who have experienced trauma.

   Online communities can offer anonymity, flexibility, and access to a wide range of perspectives and experiences. However, it's important to recognize that not all online communities may be safe or supportive, and it's important to exercise caution when engaging with online communities.

Nurturing Your Support Network:

Identifying a support network is only the first step. It's important to nurture these relationships and maintain open communication to ensure that the support is ongoing.

1. Communicate your needs: It's important to communicate your needs and expectations clearly to those in your support network. Let them know how they can help and what kind of support you need. It's also important to be open o feedback and adjust as needed. Remember that your support network can't read your mind, so don't hesitate to speak up and ask for what you need.

2. Show gratitude: Take time to express gratitude to those in your support network. Let them know how much their support means to you, and how it has helped you in your healing process. Showing appreciation can strengthen relationships and promote ongoing support.

3. Be present: It's important to be present and available for those in your support network as well. Make time to connect with them, offer support when needed, and be a good listener. Relationships are a two-way street, and it's important to show up for others as well.

4. Set boundaries: While a support network is important, it's also important to set boundaries to ensure that the relationships remain healthy and supportive. Be clear about what you are and are not comfortable with, and set limits as needed to protect your own well-being.

5. Be patient: Building and nurturing relationships takes time and effort. Don't expect your support network to be perfect or to provide all the answers. Be patient and understanding, and recognize that everyone has their own struggles and limitations.

Building and nurturing a support network is an essential part of the healing and recovery process after trauma. A support network can provide emotional and practical support, promote a sense of belonging and validation, and help individuals feel less isolated and overwhelmed. It's important to identify potential sources of support, communicate your needs clearly, show gratitude, be present for others, set boundaries, and be patient in building and nurturing relationships. With the right support in place, individuals can begin to heal and move forward after trauma.

Notes:

Chapter 6.Processing Trauma: Different Approaches to Therapy and Healing

Trauma is a complex experience that can impact a person's physical, emotional, and psychological well-being. Trauma can be caused by various events such as physical or emotional abuse, natural disasters, accidents, or witnessing violence. In order to heal from trauma, it is important to seek professional help and undergo therapy. However, there are many different approaches to trauma therapy and healing, each with its own benefits and drawbacks. This chapter will explore some of the different approaches to trauma therapy and healing.

1. **Cognitive Behavioral Therapy (CBT)**

Cognitive-behavioral therapy (CBT) is another type of therapy that can be used to treat trauma. CBT helps individuals to recognize and change negative thought patterns and behaviors that may be contributing to their trauma symptoms. The therapist works with the individual to identify and challenge their negative thoughts and beliefs and develop more positive and adaptive ways of thinking. CBT also involves practicing new coping strategies to help manage symptoms such as anxiety and flashbacks.

CBT is a type of therapy that focuses on identifying and changing negative thought patterns and behaviors. In the context of trauma therapy, CBT helps individuals learn how to cope with their trauma and manage their emotions. This can include learning relaxation techniques, identifying triggers, and challenging negative thoughts. CBT is a short-term therapy that typically involves 12-16 sessions. Cognitive-behavioral therapy (CBT) is a type of therapy that focuses on the relationship between an individual's thoughts, behaviors, and emotions. CBT aims to help individuals identify negative thoughts and behaviors that contribute to their distress and develop more positive and effective ways of coping.

CBT is a structured and goal-oriented approach to therapy that typically involves homework assignments and active participation from the individual. The therapist helps the individual identify and challenge negative thoughts, develop coping strategies, and practice new behaviors.

CBT has been found to be effective in reducing symptoms of post-traumatic stress disorder (PTSD) and other trauma-related conditions in some studies. CBT can be delivered in individual or group settings and can be adapted to meet the specific needs of each individual.

2. **Eye Movement Desensitization and Reprocessing (EMDR)**

EMDR is a type of therapy that involves reprocessing traumatic memories through a series of eye movements. This therapy is based on the idea that traumatic memories can become stuck in the brain, causing distress and emotional pain. By using eye movements, EMDR helps individuals process and integrate these traumatic memories in a way that reduces their emotional impact. EMDR can be used as a standalone therapy or in combination with other therapies.

EMDR therapy involves the use of eye movements, tapping, or other types of rhythmic stimulation to help process traumatic memories. The therapist guides the individual through a series of eye movements or other forms of stimulation while they recall their traumatic experience. This process is believed to help desensitize the individual to the traumatic memory and reduce the intensity of their emotional and physical reactions to it.

3. Dialectical Behavior Therapy (DBT)

DBT is a type of therapy that combines elements of CBT and mindfulness-based practices. DBT is often used to treat individuals with complex trauma and/or borderline personality disorder. DBT helps individuals learn how to regulate their emotions, improve their relationships, and develop coping skills. DBT can be a long-term therapy that lasts several months or even years.

4. Psychodynamic Therapy

Psychodynamic therapy is a type of therapy that focuses on exploring the unconscious thoughts and feelings that underlie a person's behavior. This therapy helps individuals gain insight into how their past experiences have shaped their current thoughts and behaviors. Psychodynamic therapy can be a longer-term therapy that lasts several years. Psychodynamic therapy is a form of therapy that focuses on exploring the individual's unconscious thoughts and emotions to help them gain insight into their behaviors and relationships. This approach to therapy is based on the idea that past experiences, particularly those from childhood, can shape an individual's current emotional and behavioral patterns.

The therapist works with the individual to explore their past experiences, emotions, and relationships and how they may be impacting their current behaviors and feelings. Psychodynamic therapy is often a longer-term approach to therapy than CBT and can involve multiple sessions per week.

Psychodynamic therapy has been found to be effective in reducing symptoms of PTSD and other trauma-related conditions in some studies. However, it may not be suitable for all individuals, and more research is needed to establish its effectiveness.

5. Trauma-Focused Cognitive Behavioral Therapy (TF-CBT)

TF-CBT is a type of therapy that is specifically designed to help children and adolescents who have experienced trauma. TF-CBT is similar to traditional CBT but is adapted to meet the unique needs of children and adolescents. This therapy involves teaching coping skills, identifying triggers, and addressing negative thought patterns. TF-CBT typically involves 12-16 sessions.

6. Somatic Experiencing

Somatic Experiencing is a type of therapy that focuses on the physiological responses to trauma. This therapy helps individuals learn how to regulate their nervous system and release stored trauma energy. Somatic Experiencing involves physical exercises and body awareness techniques. This therapy can be used as a standalone therapy or in combination with other therapies. Somatic therapy is an approach to therapy that focuses on the relationship between the body and the mind. This approach to therapy recognizes that trauma can be stored in the body and can impact an individual's physical and emotional well-being.

Somatic therapy includes various techniques such as body-centered mindfulness, movement therapy, and touch therapy. The goal of somatic therapy is to help individuals become more aware of the physical sensations associated with trauma and to develop ways of regulating these sensations.

Somatic therapy has been found to be effective in reducing symptoms of PTSD and other trauma-related conditions in some studies. It can be delivered in individual or group settings and can be adapted to meet the specific needs of each individual.

7. Art Therapy

Art therapy is a type of therapy that involves using art as a means of expression and healing. Art therapy can help individuals process their trauma in a non-verbal way, which can be especially helpful for those who have difficulty verbalizing their emotions. This therapy can involve drawing, painting, or other forms of artistic expression.

8. Narrative Therapy

Narrative therapy is a type of therapy that focuses on the stories we tell ourselves about our lives. This therapy helps individuals reframe their traumatic experiences and develop a more positive narrative. Narrative therapy can be a short-term therapy that lasts a few months.

9. Group Therapy

Group therapy is a type of therapy that involves a group of individuals who have experienced similar traumas. Group therapy can provide a sense of community and support, as well as a safe space to share experiences and emotions. Group therapy can be a long-term therapy that lasts

10. Mindfulness-Based Therapies

Mindfulness-based therapies have been increasingly used as a treatment for trauma. These approaches aim to help people become more aware of their thoughts, feelings, and sensations, and to develop a non-judgmental and accepting attitude towards them. Mindfulness-based stress reduction (MBSR) and mindfulness-based cognitive therapy (MBCT) are two examples of this approach.

MBSR was developed by Jon Kabat-Zinn in 1979 and is a structured eight-week program that combines mindfulness meditation and yoga practices. Mindfulness-based therapies may also be effective in treating trauma. These therapies, such as Mindfulness-Based Stress Reduction (MBSR) and Mindfulness-Based Cognitive Therapy (MBCT), teach individuals to focus on the present moment and to accept their thoughts and feelings without judgment. By learning to be present and mindful in the moment, individuals can learn to manage their trauma symptoms and reduce their distress.

In addition to these formal therapies, there are also a number of self-help strategies that individuals can use to process and heal from trauma. These strategies may include journaling, creative expression, exercise, and relaxation techniques such as deep breathing and meditation. It is important to note that while these self-help strategies can be beneficial, they should not be used as a replacement for formal therapy if it is needed.

 Different approaches to therapy and healing can be used, including psychotherapy, medication, and self-help strategies. It is important for individuals to work with a qualified therapist or healthcare professional to determine which approach is best suited to their unique needs and circumstances. With time, patience, and support, it is possible to overcome trauma and achieve a sense of peace and healing.

Notes:

Chapter 7 : Grief and Loss: Navigating Emotions in the Aftermath of Trauma

Grief and loss are common experiences in the aftermath of trauma. Traumatic events can cause significant emotional pain and can lead to feelings of sadness, anger, guilt, and despair. These emotions are a normal response to loss and can make it difficult to cope with the aftermath of a traumatic event. Understanding the grieving process and the emotions that come with it can help individuals navigate their emotions and move towards healing.

The grieving process is not a linear or predictable journey. It can be influenced by many factors, including culture, religion, personality, and the nature of the loss. However, there are some common stages of grief that many people experience. These stages were first proposed by Elisabeth Kubler-Ross in her book "On Death and Dying," and they include denial, anger, bargaining, depression, and acceptance.

Denial is often the first stage of grief, and it involves disbelief and shock that the loss has occurred. It can be difficult to accept the reality of the situation, and some individuals may feel numb or detached from their emotions. Anger is the second stage of grief and can be directed towards oneself, others, or even a higher power. It is a normal response to the injustice of the situation and the feeling of powerlessness that can come with it.

Bargaining is the third stage of grief, and it involves attempting to make deals with a higher power or fate to undo the loss. This can manifest as thoughts or statements such as "If only I had done this differently, then maybe this wouldn't have happened." Depression is the fourth stage of grief, and it can involve feelings of sadness, loneliness, guilt, and despair. It is important to note that depression is a common and normal response to loss and is not the same as clinical depression.

Finally, acceptance is the fifth stage of grief, and it involves coming to terms with the reality of the loss and finding a way to move forward. This does not mean that the person forgets about the loss or that they stop feeling sad, but rather that they have found a way to integrate the loss into their life and find meaning in the experience.

Grief and loss are inevitable aspects of life, but they can be especially challenging in the aftermath of trauma. Traumatic events can cause intense feelings of grief and loss, whether it be the loss of a loved one, a sense of safety and security, or a loss of trust in oneself and others. Navigating these emotions can be overwhelming and difficult, but it is an essential part of the healing process.

In the aftermath of trauma, it is common for individuals to experience a wide range of emotions, including grief, sadness, anger, and guilt. These emotions can be intense and difficult to manage, but it is important to remember that they are a natural part of the healing process.

Suppressing or ignoring these emotions can delay the healing process and cause further emotional distress.

One common aspect of grief and loss after trauma is survivor guilt. Survivor guilt is a common response to trauma, especially when others did not survive or suffered more severe consequences. Survivors may feel guilty for not doing enough to prevent the traumatic event or for surviving while others did not. It is important for survivors to recognize that they are not responsible for the actions of others and that it is okay to focus on their own healing.

Trauma can often involve experiences of grief and loss, which can be a significant emotional burden to navigate. Grief is a natural response to loss, and it is important for individuals to allow themselves time to grieve and process their emotions. There are a variety of emotions that can arise during the grieving process, including sadness, anger, guilt, and despair. However, it is important to recognize that these emotions are a normal part of the grieving process and that it is possible to move forward from them.

One approach to navigating grief and loss in the aftermath of trauma is through grief counseling or therapy. Grief therapy can provide a supportive environment for individuals to express and process their emotions related to their trauma and loss. It can also help individuals to develop coping strategies and learn skills to manage their emotions.

Another approach to navigating grief and loss is through support groups. Support groups can provide individuals with a safe and supportive environment to connect with others who have experienced similar losses. These groups can help individuals to feel less isolated in their grief and provide a space to share their experiences and emotions.

Self-care is also an important aspect of navigating grief and loss. This can include engaging in activities that promote self-compassion and self-acceptance, such as journaling, meditation, or exercise. It is important to take time to rest and prioritize self-care, as the process of grieving can be emotionally and physically exhausting.

Additionally, it is important to seek out resources and support systems that can help individuals navigate their grief and loss. This may include connecting with friends and family, seeking out community resources, or working with a grief counselor or therapist. It is important for individuals to recognize that it is okay to seek support and that they do not have to navigate their grief and loss alone.

It is also important to recognize that grief is a process that is unique to each individual. There is no "right" or "wrong" way to grieve, and it is important for individuals to give themselves permission to grieve in their own way and at their own pace.

Another important aspect of navigating grief and loss is to acknowledge and honor the memory of the person or experience that has been lost. This may include creating a memorial or engaging in rituals that hold significance for the individual. Honoring the memory of the person or experience can be a meaningful way to work through the grieving process and find a sense of closure.

It is important to note that grief and loss can also trigger symptoms of trauma. For individuals who have experienced trauma, the experience of loss can be particularly triggering and can exacerbate symptoms such as anxiety, depression, and flashbacks. It is important for individuals to work with a qualified therapist or healthcare professional to address any symptoms related to trauma that may arise during the grieving process.

Furthermore, grief and loss are an important aspect of the aftermath of trauma. Navigating these emotions can be a challenging and complex process, but there are a variety of approaches and resources that can help individuals work through their grief and find a sense of healing and closure. Grief counseling or therapy, support groups, self-care, and honoring the memory of the person or experience can all be effective tools in navigating the emotions associated with grief and loss. It is important for individuals to prioritize their emotional well-being and seek out support and resources as needed.

 Moving forward from grief and loss after trauma is a process that can take time and may require different strategies for different individuals. Here are some general steps that survivors can take towards healing:

1. Acknowledge and accept the reality of the loss: It can be tempting to deny or avoid the reality of a loss, but this can prolong the grieving process. It is important to acknowledge and accept the reality of the loss, and to allow oneself to feel the range of emotions that come with it.

2. Express and share emotions: It is important to find healthy ways to express and share one's emotions. This can include talking to a trusted friend or therapist, writing in a journal, or engaging in creative activities like art or music.

3. Practice self-care: Grieving can take a physical toll on the body, so it is important to prioritize self-care. This can include getting enough sleep, eating well, exercising, and engaging in activities that bring joy and relaxation.

4. Seek professional support: It can be helpful to work with a therapist or counselor who has experience in working with trauma and grief. They can provide a safe space to process emotions, offer tools and techniques for coping, and help with developing a plan for moving forward.

5. Find meaning and purpose: While it may seem difficult to find meaning in the aftermath of a traumatic loss, it can be helpful to focus on finding a sense of purpose or meaning in one's life. This can involve exploring one's values and goals, finding ways to give back to the community, or engaging in activities that bring a sense of purpose and fulfillment.

6. Build and maintain social support: Building and maintaining social support is important for moving forward after a loss. This can involve reaching out to friends and family for support, attending support groups or grief counseling, and finding ways to connect with others who have experienced similar losses.

7. Practice patience and self-compassion: Healing from grief and loss after trauma can take time, and it is important to practice patience and self-compassion throughout the process. It is okay to take breaks and allow oneself to feel a range of emotions without judgment or self-criticism.

In addition to these steps, it is important for individuals to remember that grief and loss are unique experiences, and there is no one "right" way to heal. It is important for individuals to find the strategies and support that work best for them and to prioritize their own healing and well-being.

Notes:

Chapter 8. The Role of Resilience: How to Cultivate and Strengthen Your Inner Strength

The experience of trauma can be incredibly difficult and can leave lasting effects on an individual's mental health and wellbeing. However, it is important to note that many individuals are able to overcome these challenges and develop resilience in the face of adversity. Resilience can be defined as the ability to adapt and bounce back in the face of adversity, and it is a crucial component in the healing process after trauma. In this chapter, we will explore the role of resilience in the aftermath of trauma, as well as how individuals can cultivate and strengthen their inner strength.

The Role of Resilience plays a critical role in helping individuals recover from trauma. Studies have found that individuals who have higher levels of resilience are more likely to experience positive outcomes after a traumatic event. For example, they may have lower rates of post-traumatic stress disorder (PTSD), depression, and anxiety. Resilience can help individuals cope with the challenges of trauma by providing them with the ability to bounce back from setbacks and persevere in the face of adversity.

There are several key factors that contribute to resilience. One of these is having a strong support system. This can include family, friends, or mental health professionals who can offer emotional support and practical assistance. Additionally, having a sense of purpose or meaning in life can help individuals maintain a sense of hope and optimism in the face of adversity. Finally, individuals who are able to regulate their emotions and maintain a positive outlook on life are more likely to develop resilience.

Cultivating and Strengthening Your Inner Strength While some individuals may have a natural inclination towards resilience, it is possible to cultivate and strengthen your inner strength even if you do not consider yourself a particularly resilient person. Here are some strategies that can help:

1. Build a Support System: As mentioned earlier, having a strong support system is critical for developing resilience. Make an effort to connect with others who can offer emotional support and practical assistance.

2. Practice Self-Care: Taking care of yourself is crucial in building resilience. Make sure to prioritize activities that promote your physical and mental health, such as exercise, healthy eating, and getting enough sleep.

3. Develop Coping Skills: Coping skills are techniques and strategies that help individuals manage stress and difficult emotions. Examples include deep breathing exercises, meditation, or mindfulness practices.

4. Engage in Meaningful Activities: Finding activities that provide a sense of purpose or meaning can help individuals maintain hope and optimism in the face of adversity. This can include hobbies, volunteering, or pursuing a career or education.

5. Seek Professional Help: While building resilience is possible on your own, seeking professional help can provide additional support and guidance. A mental health professional can help you develop coping skills and offer strategies for managing difficult emotions.

Resilience is the ability to bounce back and adapt to adversity, including traumatic experiences. Developing resilience can help individuals cope with the aftermath of trauma and promote a sense of well-being. According to Bonanno and Mancini (2012), resilience is a dynamic process that involves the interaction of multiple factors, including personal characteristics, social support, and coping strategies.

One key factor in developing resilience is having a positive mindset. In his book "Man's Search for Meaning," Viktor Frankl writes about his experiences as a Holocaust survivor and the importance of finding meaning and purpose in life. Frankl believed that having a sense of purpose and meaning can help individuals overcome even the most difficult challenges.

Another important factor in developing resilience is social support. Having a strong support network of family, friends, and community can provide a sense of belonging, validation, and emotional support during difficult times. Social support can also help individuals access practical assistance, such as financial support, transportation, and child care (Norris et al., 2009).

Coping strategies are also crucial in building resilience. Coping strategies can include problem-solving, emotion-focused coping, and avoidance coping. Problem-solving involves actively seeking solutions to the problem at hand, while emotion-focused coping involves managing the emotional impact of the stressor. Avoidance coping, on the other hand, involves avoiding the stressor altogether. While avoidance coping may provide temporary relief, it can ultimately lead to greater distress in the long run (Bonanno & Mancini, 2012).

Mindfulness-based practices have also been shown to be effective in building resilience. Mindfulness involves being present in the moment and accepting one's experiences without judgment. Studies have shown that mindfulness-based interventions can reduce symptoms of depression and anxiety and improve overall well-being (Keng et al., 2011).

Another important aspect of building resilience is self-compassion. Self-compassion involves treating oneself with kindness, understanding, and acceptance, even in the face of difficult emotions or experiences. Research has shown that self-compassion is associated with greater resilience, lower levels of anxiety and depression, and better overall mental health (Neff, 2009).

Example : Trauma from Natural Disasters

Trauma from natural disasters can result in a range of psychological symptoms, such as anxiety, depression, and PTSD. Natural disasters can be caused by events such as hurricanes, earthquakes, floods, and wildfires.

One potential method for overcoming trauma from natural disasters is through therapy, such as cognitive-behavioral therapy (CBT) or mindfulness-based stress reduction (MBSR). CBT involves identifying and challenging negative thoughts and beliefs related to the trauma, while MBSR involves developing mindfulness skills to reduce stress and improve overall well-being. Both CBT and MBSR are evidence-based treatments that have been shown to be effective in treating trauma. Natural disasters can be traumatic experiences that lead to a range of mental health issues. However, with proper support and resources, survivors can achieve healing and resilience. A study by Norris et al. (2009) evaluated the effectiveness of a community-based intervention called the Katrina Assessment and Treatment Program (KATP) for survivors of Hurricane Katrina. The program provided mental health services, case management, and other resources to support survivors in their recovery. The study found that participants who received KATP services had significantly reduced symptoms of PTSD, depression, and anxiety.

Another study by Larkin et al. (2016) evaluated the effectiveness of a mindfulness-based intervention for survivors of the 2011 Joplin tornado. The intervention involved mindfulness meditation and other practices to promote emotional regulation and resilience. The study found that participants who completed the intervention had significantly reduced symptoms of PTSD, depression, and anxiety and improved overall well-being.

These studies demonstrate that survivors of natural disasters can achieve healing and resilience with the appropriate support and resources.

Other therapy methods for overcoming trauma from natural disasters include seeking support from family and friends, engaging in physical activity, and participating in activities that promote a sense of community and purpose. It can also be helpful to practice self-care, such as getting enough rest, eating a healthy diet, and engaging in activities that bring joy and relaxation.

In summary, developing resilience after trauma involves a combination of personal characteristics, social support, coping strategies, mindfulness, and self-compassion. Building resilience is a dynamic process that requires ongoing effort and attention, but can ultimately lead to greater well-being and a sense of inner strength in the face of adversity. The experience of trauma can be incredibly difficult, but it is possible to develop resilience and inner strength in the aftermath. Building a support system, practicing self-care, developing coping skills, engaging in meaningful activities, and seeking professional help can all contribute to the development of resilience. While the journey to healing may not be easy, it is important to remember that it is possible to overcome the challenges of trauma and emerge stronger on the other side.

Notes:

Chapter 9 :Forgiveness and Moving Forward: Finding Closure After Trauma

Trauma can have a significant impact on a person's life. It can cause emotional and psychological distress, leading to long-lasting effects. One of the most challenging aspects of trauma is finding closure and moving forward. Forgiveness can play a crucial role in this process. In this chapter, we will explore the concept of forgiveness and its relationship with finding closure after trauma.

What is Forgiveness?

Forgiveness is a complex and multifaceted concept that has been studied extensively in the field of psychology. At its core, forgiveness involves a decision to let go of resentment, anger, and the desire for revenge towards the person or situation that caused harm. Forgiveness does not mean forgetting what happened or excusing the behavior of the person who caused the harm. Instead, it involves acknowledging the harm done, accepting the reality of the situation, and choosing to let go of negative emotions associated with the event.

The Role of Forgiveness in Healing from Trauma

Forgiveness can play a crucial role in the healing process after trauma. When individuals hold onto anger and resentment towards the person or situation that caused harm, it can prevent them from moving forward and finding closure. Holding onto negative emotions can also lead to physical health problems, including increased levels of stress, anxiety, and depression. Forgiveness can help individuals let go of negative emotions and find peace, leading to improved mental and physical health.

Studies have found that forgiveness is associated with several positive outcomes, including reduced levels of stress and anxiety, improved mood, increased self-esteem, and better interpersonal relationships (Worthington et al., 2007). Forgiveness can also improve physical health outcomes, including lower blood pressure and decreased risk of heart disease (Toussaint et al., 2015). Forgiveness can also improve the quality of life for individuals who have experienced trauma.

Types of Forgiveness

There are several types of forgiveness that individuals can choose to engage in, depending on their specific needs and the nature of the trauma. These include:

1. Decisional Forgiveness: This type of forgiveness involves a conscious decision to let go of negative emotions towards the person or situation that caused harm. It does not necessarily involve feelings of forgiveness but is a choice to release negative emotions.

2. Emotional Forgiveness: Emotional forgiveness involves actively working towards replacing negative emotions with positive emotions, including empathy and compassion towards the person or situation that caused harm.

3. Relational Forgiveness: This type of forgiveness involves repairing or rebuilding the relationship between the victim and the perpetrator. It involves working towards reconciliation and restoring trust.

4. Self-Forgiveness: Self-forgiveness involves letting go of negative emotions towards oneself for any perceived mistakes or faults. It involves acknowledging and accepting responsibility for past actions and choosing to move forward in a positive way.

The Process of Forgiveness

The process of forgiveness can be challenging, especially for individuals who have experienced trauma. It is not a one-time event but a continuous process that requires ongoing effort and commitment. The following steps can be helpful in the forgiveness process:

1. Acknowledge the harm that was done and the negative emotions associated with it. It is essential to be honest and open about the impact of the trauma on oneself.

2. Decide to forgive. Forgiveness is a choice, and it is important to make a conscious decision to let go of negative emotions and choose forgiveness.

3. Work towards understanding the person or situation that caused harm. Empathy and understanding can be powerful tools in the forgiveness process.

4. Let go of negative emotions. This step involves actively releasing negative emotions towards the person or situation that caused harm.

5. Find meaning in the experience. Finding meaning in the trauma can be a powerful way to move forward and find closure. It involves reframing the trauma into a motivation, and finding a positive outlet.

Once you have recognized the value of forgiveness, it is important to begin the process of forgiveness. This process can be long and challenging, but it is important to stick with it in order to move forward and find closure after trauma. Here are some steps to consider as you embark on the journey towards forgiveness:

Acknowledge the pain and hurt that was caused

It is important to recognize the pain and hurt that you experienced as a result of the trauma. This acknowledgement allows you to fully understand the impact of the event on your life and why forgiveness is necessary.

Take responsibility for your own healing

Forgiveness is a personal journey and it is up to you to take responsibility for your own healing. This involves making the decision to forgive and committing to the process, even if it is difficult.

Allow yourself to feel emotions

It is important to allow yourself to feel a range of emotions, including anger, sadness, and hurt. These emotions are a natural response to the trauma and should be acknowledged and expressed in a healthy way.

Practice empathy

Empathy is the ability to understand and share the feelings of others. Practicing empathy can help you to see the situation from the perspective of the person who caused the trauma and may help to soften feelings of anger and hurt.

Consider therapy

Working with a therapist can provide valuable support and guidance as you work towards forgiveness. A therapist can help you process your emotions and work through any obstacles that may arise.

Let go of resentment

Holding onto resentment only prolongs the pain and hurt caused by the trauma. Letting go of resentment involves accepting the situation and releasing the negative emotions associated with it.

Practice self-care

Taking care of yourself physically, emotionally, and mentally is essential during the forgiveness process. This may include exercise, eating a healthy diet, getting enough sleep, and engaging in activities that bring you joy.

Focus on the present

Forgiveness involves letting go of the past and focusing on the present. This means not dwelling on the past and not allowing it to impact your current relationships and experiences.

Set boundaries

Forgiveness does not mean that you have to allow the person who caused the trauma back into your life. Setting boundaries is important in order to protect yourself and ensure that you are not further hurt.

Practice gratitude

Focusing on gratitude can help shift your perspective and increase feelings of positivity and hope. Consider keeping a gratitude journal or taking time each day to reflect on the things in your life that you are grateful for.

While forgiveness may seem like a daunting task, it is an essential part of moving forward and finding closure after trauma. By following these steps and seeking support from trusted friends, family members, or mental health professionals, you can begin the process of forgiveness and ultimately find peace and healing.

Forgiveness is a challenging but necessary process for finding closure after trauma. It involves acknowledging the pain and hurt that was caused, taking responsibility for your own healing, and practicing empathy and self-care. Seeking support from trusted friends, family members, or mental health professionals can provide valuable guidance and help you work through any obstacles that may arise. Ultimately, forgiveness allows you to let go of the past, focus on the present, and find peace and healing.

One of the biggest challenges of trauma recovery is finding closure and moving forward. This involves not only addressing the past trauma but also cultivating inner strength and resilience to cope with the challenges of the present and future. In this chapter, we will explore the concept of closure after trauma, the role of forgiveness in the healing process, and strategies for finding meaning and purpose in life after trauma.

What is Closure After Trauma?

Closure is a term that is often used in the context of grief and loss, but it can also be applied to trauma recovery. Closure refers to the process of coming to terms with a traumatic event and finding a sense of resolution and peace. It involves acceptance of the past, letting go of anger and resentment, and moving forward with a sense of purpose and meaning.

Closure after trauma is not a one-time event, but rather a gradual process that involves many different stages. It can take months or even years to achieve closure, and the journey can be difficult and painful. However, it is a necessary step in the healing process, and it can help individuals to move forward with their lives.

The Role of Forgiveness in Finding Closure

Forgiveness is a key component of finding closure after trauma. Forgiveness does not mean forgetting or condoning the actions of the person who caused the trauma. Instead, it involves letting go of anger, resentment, and bitterness towards the person who caused the trauma. Forgiveness is not easy, and it does not happen overnight. It is a process that takes time and effort, but it is a crucial step towards finding closure and moving forward.

Research has shown that forgiveness can have a positive impact on mental health and well-being. A study conducted by the Stanford Forgiveness Project found that forgiveness can lead to lower levels of anxiety, depression, and anger, and higher levels of self-esteem and overall life satisfaction (Worthington, 2005). Forgiveness has also been linked to improved relationships and greater social support (Enright & Fitzgibbons, 2000).

Forgiveness is a personal choice, and it is not always necessary or appropriate. It is important to remember that forgiveness is not a requirement for healing, and some individuals may never be able to forgive the person who caused their trauma. However, for those who are able to forgive, it can be a powerful tool for finding closure and moving forward.

Strategies for Finding Closure After Trauma

Finding closure after trauma is a complex process that involves many different strategies and techniques. Some of the most effective strategies for finding closure include:

1. Seek therapy: Working with a therapist can be an important step in finding closure after a traumatic event. A trained therapist can help you process your emotions, develop coping strategies, and work towards forgiveness and acceptance.

2. Practice self-care: Engaging in self-care activities such as exercise, meditation, and relaxation techniques can help to reduce stress and promote healing. Taking care of your physical and emotional health is an important part of the closure process.

3. Connect with others: Building and maintaining supportive relationships with family, friends, or support groups can help to provide a sense of connection and belonging, reducing feelings of isolation and loneliness.

4. Express yourself: Finding healthy ways to express your emotions, such as through journaling, art, or music, can help to release pent-up feelings and allow for greater emotional processing.

5. Challenge negative thoughts: Trauma can lead to negative self-talk and beliefs that may hinder the closure process. Challenging these thoughts and replacing them with more positive, realistic beliefs can help to promote healing and a sense of closure.

6. Forgive: Forgiveness can be a difficult but important step in finding closure after trauma. This does not mean forgetting or excusing the actions of the perpetrator, but rather releasing the hold that anger and resentment may have over your life.

7. Set realistic goals: Setting small, achievable goals can help to provide a sense of accomplishment and progress towards closure. Celebrating small victories can help to build momentum and motivation for continued healing.

8. Practice gratitude: Focusing on the positive aspects of your life, such as supportive relationships, personal strengths, and past successes, can help to shift the focus away from the trauma and towards a more hopeful future.

In conclusion, finding closure after trauma can be a difficult and complex process. It requires a willingness to confront and process emotions, build supportive relationships, and work towards forgiveness and acceptance. While closure may not mean forgetting the trauma, it can provide a sense of resolution and a path towards healing and moving forward in life. By utilizing these strategies, individuals can begin to find a sense of closure and move towards a more positive future.

Notes:

Chapter 10 : Overcoming Shame and Guilt: Letting Go of Self-Blame and Judgement

Shame and guilt are common emotional reactions to trauma. Shame is the feeling of being unworthy, inadequate or defective as a person, while guilt is the feeling of responsibility for a wrongdoing. Both can be overwhelming and make it difficult to move forward after a traumatic experience. However, it is possible to overcome shame and guilt and let go of self-blame and judgment. This chapter will explore the causes and effects of shame and guilt, as well as strategies for overcoming them.

Causes of Shame and Guilt:

Shame and guilt are complex emotions that can be caused by a variety of factors. Trauma is a common cause of shame and guilt, especially if the trauma involves harm to oneself or others. Survivors of abuse, violence, and other traumatic experiences often blame themselves for what happened, leading to feelings of shame and guilt. Additionally, society and culture can reinforce shame and guilt by creating unrealistic standards of perfection and promoting the idea that mistakes and failures are unacceptable.

Effects of Shame and Guilt:

Shame and guilt can have a profound impact on a person's mental health and well-being. Shame can lead to feelings of worthlessness and a sense of being fundamentally flawed. Guilt, on the other hand, can lead to self-punishment, self-criticism, and self-doubt. Both shame and guilt can cause a person to withdraw from others, avoid social situations, and become isolated. They can also lead to depression, anxiety, and other mental health problems.

Strategies for Overcoming Shame and Guilt:

1. Identify the Source of Shame and Guilt: The first step in overcoming shame and guilt is to identify their source. This may involve exploring the events and experiences that led to the feelings of shame and guilt. Once the source is identified, it can be easier to understand the emotions and begin to address them.

2. Challenge Negative Beliefs: Shame and guilt are often fueled by negative beliefs about oneself. These beliefs may be based on inaccurate or distorted perceptions of the self. To overcome shame and guilt, it is important to challenge these negative beliefs and replace them with more positive and accurate ones. This can be done through cognitive-behavioral therapy, which helps to identify and modify negative thought patterns.

3. Practice Self-Compassion:

Practicing self-compassion can be an effective way to overcome shame and guilt. Self-compassion involves treating yourself with kindness, understanding, and acceptance. It is essential to remind yourself that you are not alone in your experience and that it is okay to be imperfect.

4. Seek Support:

Seeking support from loved ones, friends, or a therapist can be an essential step in overcoming shame and guilt. Having a support system can provide a safe and non-judgmental space to talk about your feelings and experiences. A therapist can also help you develop coping strategies and work through feelings of shame and guilt.

5. Practice Forgiveness:

Forgiveness is a crucial aspect of letting go of self-blame and judgment. Forgiving oneself can be challenging, but it is essential to acknowledge that you did the best you could at the time. Forgiveness also involves accepting that what happened was not your fault and that you are not to blame.

6. Engage in Activities That Bring You Joy:

Engaging in activities that bring you joy can be an effective way to overcome shame and guilt. Doing things that make you happy

One of the most common challenges that people face after experiencing trauma is negative thinking. Negative thoughts and beliefs can lead to feelings of hopelessness, helplessness, and despair, which can make it challenging to move forward and find healing. In this chapter, we will explore the impact of negative thinking on trauma survivors and strategies for avoiding negative thoughts associated with trauma.

The Impact of Negative Thinking on Trauma Survivors

Negative thinking is common after experiencing trauma. Trauma can shatter an individual's sense of safety and control, leading to feelings of vulnerability and powerlessness. These feelings can then lead to negative thoughts and beliefs, such as "I'm not good enough," "I'm weak," or "I'm to blame for what happened." These thoughts can create a negative spiral of self-blame and self-criticism, which can lead to depression, anxiety, and other mental health issues.

Negative thinking can also lead to a heightened sense of fear and anxiety. After experiencing trauma, it's common for individuals to experience hyper-vigilance, where they are constantly on guard and anticipating danger. Negative thoughts and beliefs can exacerbate this hyper-vigilance and make it challenging to relax and feel safe.

Strategies for Avoiding Negative Thoughts Associated with Trauma

1. Challenge Negative Thoughts

The first step in avoiding negative thoughts associated with trauma is to challenge them. Negative thoughts are often automatic and can be challenging to recognize. However, by paying attention to your thoughts and challenging negative ones, you can start to reframe your thinking.

To challenge negative thoughts, ask yourself the following questions:

- Is this thought true?

- What evidence do I have to support this thought?

- Is this thought helpful?

- What would I say to a friend who had this thought?

By challenging negative thoughts, you can start to recognize when you're engaging in negative thinking patterns and replace them with more positive and helpful thoughts.

2. Practice Mindfulness

Mindfulness is the practice of being present and non-judgmental in the moment. It's a helpful tool for avoiding negative thoughts associated with trauma because it can help you stay grounded and connected to the present moment. Mindfulness can also help you recognize when negative thoughts are arising and give you the space to challenge them.

To practice mindfulness, try the following:

- Focus on your breath: Take a few deep breaths and focus on the sensation of air moving in and out of your body.

- Notice your surroundings: Pay attention to the sights, sounds, and sensations around you.

- Stay present: When your mind starts to wander, gently bring your attention back to the present moment.

3. Engage in Positive Activities

Engaging in positive activities can help counteract negative thoughts associated with trauma. Positive activities can be anything that brings you joy or a sense of accomplishment, such as exercise, hobbies, or spending time with loved ones. By engaging in positive activities, you can create positive experiences that can help counteract negative thoughts and feelings.

Negative thinking is a common challenge for trauma survivors. However, by challenging negative thoughts, practicing mindfulness, engaging in positive activities, and seeking support, individuals can avoid negative thoughts associated with trauma and find healing. It's important to remember that healing from trauma is a process, and it's okay to seek support and take the time you need to heal. By implementing these strategies and seeking support, individuals

Emotional triggers are reminders of the traumatic experience, which can result in an emotional response, such as fear, anxiety, or anger. These triggers can occur at any time and in any situation, making it difficult for individuals to function in their daily lives. Fortunately, there are steps that individuals can take to overcome traumatic emotional triggers and reduce their impact on daily life.

One effective strategy for overcoming traumatic emotional triggers is to identify and understand them. Individuals who have experienced trauma should take the time to recognize their triggers, including what they are and when they tend to occur. This can help individuals prepare for these triggers and develop strategies for coping with them when they arise. Additionally, identifying triggers can help individuals avoid situations that may cause an emotional response, reducing the likelihood of being triggered.

An effective strategy for overcoming traumatic emotional triggers is to practice grounding techniques. Grounding techniques involve bringing one's attention to the present moment and focusing on the physical sensations of the body. This can help individuals feel more connected to their surroundings and reduce the impact of emotional triggers. Examples of grounding techniques include deep breathing, progressive muscle relaxation, and mindfulness meditation.

Chapter 11: Empowering Yourself: Reclaiming Your Identity After Trauma

A person's sense of self and identity can be destroyed through trauma. Those who go through this experience could feel entirely alienated from their identity, helplessness, and power. But following trauma, it is possible to reestablish a feeling of self and personal strength. In this chapter, we'll look at self-empowerment techniques and identity recovery following trauma.

Understanding How Trauma Affects Identity

Experiencing trauma can have a significant impact on one's sense of self. People may feel as though they have lost themselves or their sense of purpose after experiencing trauma. For those who have gone through catastrophic experiences that have irrevocably changed their lives, such as a physical injury, this loss can be very difficult.

An individual may occasionally feel alienated from their sense of self after a traumatic event. They might believe they have changed from the person they were prior to the terrible occurrence. This may be especially true for people who suffered trauma as children or who were wronged by someone they trusted.

After trauma, regaining one's sense of self is an essential step in the healing process. It is crucial to understand that rebuilding requires time and patience. It could also call for a readiness to be receptive to fresh insights and experiences.

Taking charge of your life and making choices that are consistent with your values and objectives are key to empowerment. It is crucial to recovering your sense of self following trauma. These are some techniques for taking control of your life following trauma:

Concentrate on your controllable actions:

Trauma can make a person feel as though they have no control over their lives. You may reclaim your sense of power and agency by concentrating on the things you can manage. Setting modest objectives for yourself or acting on critical topics to you may be part of this.

Take care of your physical, emotional, and mental wellbeing by engaging in self-care. exercising or spending time with loved ones are examples of activities that make you feel good.

After a traumatic event, support from family members or a therapist can be incredibly helpful. Discussing your feelings and experiences with others might help you digest what has happened and create a strategy for the future.

Trauma can leave people with low self-esteem and self-confidence. You can regain your sense of self and proceed by challenging these beliefs and swapping them out for more uplifting and empowering ideas.

Reclaiming your identity after trauma involves rediscovering who you are and what is important to you. Here are some strategies for reclaiming your identity after trauma:

Survivors may be fearful of taking risks or trying new things because they have experienced the consequences of vulnerability in the past. This fear can lead to avoidance behavior and a lack of self-growth. In order to overcome this fear, it may be helpful to engage in exposure therapy, where survivors gradually expose themselves to the feared situation in a safe and controlled environment. This can help survivors build confidence and a sense of mastery over their fear, leading to increased empowerment and identity reclamation.

Another important step in empowering oneself and reclaiming one's identity after trauma is self-compassion. Survivors often struggle with self-blame and self-criticism, which can hinder their ability to see themselves in a positive light and move forward. Practicing self-compassion involves treating oneself with the same kindness, concern, and support one would offer to a good friend in need. This can involve self-talk that is kind and understanding, acknowledging that everyone makes mistakes and that it is normal to struggle after a traumatic event. Research has shown that practicing self-compassion can increase resilience, decrease symptoms of anxiety and depression, and promote well-being (Neff, 2011).

In addition to self-compassion, survivors can benefit from building a sense of community and connection. Trauma can lead to feelings of isolation and disconnection, which can hinder the process of empowerment and identity reclamation. It is important for survivors to seek out supportive relationships and engage in activities that promote social connection. This can involve joining support groups, participating in community events, or volunteering for a cause that is meaningful to them. By building a sense of community and connection, survivors can gain a sense of belonging and purpose, which can contribute to their overall well-being.

Overall, empowering oneself and reclaiming one's identity after trauma can be a challenging process, but it is possible with the right support and resources. By taking small steps towards self-compassion, facing fears, building a sense of community, and practicing resilience, survivors can move towards a sense of empowerment and identity reclamation. It is important for survivors to remember that healing is a journey and that everyone's path is unique. With patience, self-care, and perseverance, survivors can find their own way towards healing and a sense of empowerment after trauma.

Chapter 12 : Finding Meaning and Purpose: Using Trauma to Inspire Positive Change

In this chapter, we will explore the concept of finding meaning and purpose after trauma and discuss how it can lead to personal growth and empowerment.

Finding meaning and purpose after trauma can be a long and difficult process, but it is crucial for individuals to move forward and create a new narrative for themselves. Research suggests that finding meaning after a traumatic event is associated with better mental health outcomes, including lower levels of depression and anxiety (Park, 2010). Additionally, individuals who find meaning in their trauma report greater satisfaction with life and a stronger sense of purpose (Calhoun & Tedeschi, 2006).

One way to find meaning and purpose after trauma is to focus on personal growth and transformation. Trauma can be a catalyst for personal growth and can lead individuals to reevaluate their priorities and values. By focusing on personal growth, individuals can use their trauma as an opportunity to develop resilience, strengthen relationships, and enhance their overall well-being.

Another way to find meaning and purpose after trauma is to engage in activities that align with one's values and beliefs. Research suggests that engaging in activities that are meaningful to individuals can help them find a sense of purpose and direction in life (Sheldon & Kasser, 2008). For example, volunteering for a cause that is important to an individual can provide a sense of purpose and can help them feel like they are making a difference in the world.

In addition to focusing on personal growth and engaging in meaningful activities, it is important for individuals to reframe their trauma and view it as an opportunity for positive change. Reframing the trauma involves changing the way an individual thinks about the event and finding a new perspective on the experience. This can involve focusing on the positive aspects of the experience, such as the strength and resilience that were developed as a result of the trauma.

It is also important for individuals to seek support from others as they navigate the process of finding meaning and purpose after trauma. This can include professional therapy, support groups, or connecting with friends and family members who are empathetic and understanding. Support from others can help individuals feel validated, understood, and less alone in their journey.

It is important for individuals to practice self-compassion and forgiveness as they work to find meaning and purpose after trauma. Self-compassion involves treating oneself with kindness and understanding, and forgiving oneself for any perceived mistakes or shortcomings. This can help individuals overcome feelings of guilt, shame, and self-blame that may be associated with their trauma and can allow them to move forward in a positive direction.

In conclusion, finding meaning and purpose after trauma is a crucial step towards personal growth and empowerment. It involves focusing on personal growth and transformation, engaging in activities that align with one's values and beliefs, reframing the trauma, seeking support from others, and practicing self-compassion and forgiveness. While the process of finding meaning and purpose after trauma can be challenging, it is possible and can lead to a sense of fulfillment, purpose, and overall well-being.

Finding Meaning and Purpose, Using Trauma to Inspire Positive Change

Trauma can shake our very sense of meaning and purpose, leaving us feeling lost, confused, and adrift. However, with time, reflection, and healing, it is possible to find new meaning and purpose in life, often fueled by the very experiences that once seemed to threaten our existence. In fact, many people who have experienced trauma report feeling a sense of growth and positive change, known as post-traumatic growth (PTG), which can lead to greater resilience, self-awareness, and appreciation for life.

Finding meaning and purpose after trauma can be a challenging but rewarding journey. Here are some strategies to help you use your experiences to inspire positive change and find new direction in life:

1. Reflect on your values and beliefs: Take time to reflect on what is most important to you in life. What do you believe in? What do you value? What are your passions? Trauma can sometimes lead us to question our values and beliefs, but it can also help us clarify and reaffirm them.

2. Find ways to give back: One way to find meaning and purpose is by giving back to others. Helping others can provide a sense of fulfillment and meaning, and can also help you feel connected to something larger than yourself. Consider volunteering for a cause you care about or getting involved in your community.

3. Pursue your interests: Trauma can sometimes leave us feeling like we've lost our sense of self or our passion for life. Take time to explore your interests and hobbies, and consider pursuing them more fully. Engaging in activities you enjoy can help you feel more connected to yourself and the world around you.

4. Seek out positive role models: Surround yourself with people who inspire you and embody the qualities you admire. Positive role models can help you feel more empowered and motivated to pursue your goals and dreams.

5. Practice self-compassion: Trauma can often lead to feelings of self-blame, guilt, and shame. Practicing self-compassion can help you overcome these negative self-talk patterns and cultivate a more positive and supportive inner voice. Be kind and gentle with yourself, and remember that healing takes time.

6. Set goals and take action: Setting goals and taking action towards them can help you feel more motivated and empowered. Start small and work your way up to bigger goals, and be sure to celebrate your progress along the way.

7. Connect with others who have experienced trauma: Connecting with others who have experienced trauma can help you feel less alone and more understood. Joining a support group or seeking therapy can provide a safe space to share your experiences and learn from others.

It is important to note that finding meaning and purpose after trauma is a highly personal and individual process. What works for one person may not work for another, and there is no "right" way to navigate this journey. It is important to be patient and kind with yourself, and to seek professional help if needed.

Example : Childhood Trauma

Childhood trauma can have long-lasting effects on an individual's mental and emotional health. Childhood trauma can include physical, sexual, or emotional abuse, neglect, and exposure to violence. The experience of childhood trauma can result in a range of psychological symptoms, such as depression, anxiety, post-traumatic stress disorder (PTSD), and difficulties in relationships.

Overcoming Childhood Sexual Abuse

Childhood sexual abuse is a traumatic experience that can have long-lasting effects on mental health and well-being. However, with proper treatment and support, survivors can achieve healing and recovery. A study by Cloitre et al. (2010) evaluated the effectiveness of a treatment program called Skills Training in Affective and Interpersonal Regulation (STAIR) for women who had experienced childhood sexual abuse. The program focused on developing skills in emotional regulation, interpersonal relationships, and self-care. The study found that participants who completed the program had significantly reduced symptoms of post-traumatic stress disorder (PTSD) and depression and improved overall functioning.

Another study by Saxe et al. (2005) evaluated the effectiveness of trauma-focused cognitive-behavioral therapy (TF-CBT) for children who had experienced sexual abuse. TF-CBT involves a combination of cognitive-behavioral therapy and exposure therapy. The study found that children who received TF-CBT had significantly reduced symptoms of PTSD and improved overall functioning compared to those who received non-trauma-focused therapy.

These studies demonstrate that survivors of childhood sexual abuse can achieve healing and recovery with the appropriate treatment and support.

One potential method for overcoming childhood trauma is through therapy, such as trauma-focused cognitive-behavioral therapy (TF-CBT) or Eye Movement Desensitization and Reprocessing (EMDR). TF-CBT is an evidence-based treatment that has been shown to be effective in treating childhood trauma. It involves teaching coping skills, processing traumatic memories, and addressing negative thoughts and beliefs. EMDR is another therapy that has been shown to be effective in treating trauma. It involves using eye movements or other forms of bilateral stimulation to help the brain process traumatic memories and reduce associated distress.

Other methods for overcoming childhood trauma include self-care practices, such as exercise, meditation, and spending time in nature. It can also be helpful to connect with a support group or to participate in activities that promote a sense of community.

Example : Trauma from Combat

Trauma from combat can result in a range of psychological symptoms, such as PTSD, depression, and anxiety. Combat trauma can be caused by exposure to life-threatening events, witnessing death and injury, and being away from home and family for extended periods.

One potential method for overcoming combat trauma is through therapy, such as cognitive processing therapy (CPT) or prolonged exposure therapy (PE). CPT involves identifying and challenging negative thoughts and beliefs related to the trauma, while PE involves gradually confronting the trauma through exposure to reminders of the traumatic event. Both CPT and PE are evidence-based treatments that have been shown to be effective in treating combat trauma. Combat trauma is a common experience for military personnel, and it can lead to PTSD and other mental health issues. However, with proper treatment and support, many veterans can achieve successful recovery. A study by Watkins et al. (2011) evaluated the effectiveness of prolonged exposure therapy (PE) for veterans with PTSD related to combat trauma. PE involves repeated exposure to traumatic memories in a safe and controlled environment. The study found that participants who completed PE had significantly reduced symptoms of PTSD and improved overall functioning.

Another study by Monson et al. (2006) evaluated the effectiveness of cognitive processing therapy (CPT) for veterans with PTSD related to combat trauma. CPT involves challenging and changing negative thoughts related to the traumatic event. The study found that participants who completed CPT had significantly reduced symptoms of PTSD and improved overall functioning compared to those who received a non-trauma-focused therapy.

These studies demonstrate that veterans with combat trauma can achieve successful recovery with the appropriate treatment and support.

In addition to therapy, other methods for overcoming combat trauma include physical activity, such as running or weightlifting, and participating in creative activities, such as writing or art. It can also be helpful to connect with other veterans or individuals who have experienced trauma and to participate in activities that promote a sense of community and purpose.

Notes:

Chapter 13 : Long-Term Healing: Living Fully Beyond Trauma

Long-term healing after trauma is a complex process that requires ongoing efforts and commitment. While trauma can have significant impacts on one's physical, emotional, and mental health, it is possible to live fully beyond trauma. The journey towards long-term healing involves a combination of therapeutic interventions, self-care practices, and a positive mindset. This article aims to explore some of the key factors that contribute to long-term healing after trauma and provide practical tips for individuals who are struggling with the aftermath of trauma.

One of the essential steps towards long-term healing after trauma is seeking professional help. Trauma therapy is an evidence-based treatment that can help individuals cope with the emotional and psychological impacts of trauma. Trauma-focused therapies, such as Cognitive Behavioral Therapy (CBT), Eye Movement Desensitization and Reprocessing (EMDR), and Prolonged Exposure (PE) therapy, have been found to be effective in treating trauma-related symptoms, including anxiety, depression, and PTSD (Post Traumatic Stress Disorder). These therapies can help individuals process traumatic experiences, learn coping skills, and develop a sense of control over their lives.

Self-care is another critical factor that contributes to long-term healing after trauma. Self-care involves engaging in activities that promote physical, emotional, and mental well-being. Some self-care practices that can be helpful for individuals who have experienced trauma include mindfulness meditation, yoga, exercise, spending time in nature, journaling, and spending time with loved ones. Self-care practices can help individuals manage stress, reduce symptoms of anxiety and depression, and improve overall well-being.

Building and maintaining healthy relationships is also crucial for long-term healing after trauma. Trauma can lead to feelings of isolation and disconnection from others. However, connecting with supportive individuals can help individuals feel understood, validated, and cared for. It is essential to cultivate healthy relationships with people who are empathetic, non-judgmental, and supportive. Friends, family members, support groups, and mental health professionals can all provide valuable support and understanding to individuals who have experienced trauma.

Another important aspect of long-term healing after trauma is cultivating a positive mindset. Trauma can lead to negative beliefs about oneself, others, and the world. These negative beliefs can contribute to feelings of hopelessness, helplessness, and despair. However, cultivating a positive mindset can help individuals find meaning and purpose in life and move towards a more fulfilling and satisfying life. Some strategies for cultivating a positive mindset include practicing gratitude, engaging in positive self-talk, setting achievable goals, and focusing on one's strengths and abilities.

Living Fully Beyond trauma is a process of healing and growth after a traumatic experience, which involves creating a new sense of meaning, purpose, and joy in life. It is important to note that recovery from trauma is a unique and personal journey, and the outcomes may vary from one individual to another. In this response, we will discuss two examples of successful Living Fully Beyond trauma experiences and their outcomes.

Example : Overcoming Childhood Trauma

Mary, a 35-year-old woman, experienced severe physical and emotional abuse from her father during her childhood. As a result, she developed low self-esteem, anxiety, depression, and trust issues. Mary sought help from a therapist and started her journey towards Living Fully Beyond trauma. The therapist used trauma-focused cognitive-behavioral therapy (TF-CBT) to help Mary process her traumatic experiences and learn coping strategies. The therapy also focused on rebuilding her self-esteem and trust in others. Mary also joined a support group for survivors of childhood trauma, where she found validation and support from others who had gone through similar experiences.

Through her therapy and support group, Mary was able to create a new sense of meaning and purpose in life. She pursued a degree in social work and started working with children who had experienced trauma. Mary also engaged in hobbies such as painting and hiking, which brought her joy and a sense of accomplishment. With time, Mary was able to heal from her childhood trauma and no longer felt defined by it. She was able to live a fulfilling life and form healthy relationships with others.

Example: Recovering from a Natural Disaster

In 2017, Hurricane Harvey hit Houston, Texas, causing widespread destruction and trauma. Lisa, a 42-year-old mother of two, lost her home and all her possessions in the hurricane. She and her family were forced to live in a shelter for several weeks, which was a traumatic experience for her and her children. After the hurricane, Lisa sought help from a therapist and started her journey towards Living Fully Beyond trauma. The therapist used Eye Movement Desensitization and Reprocessing (EMDR) therapy to help Lisa process her traumatic experiences and alleviate her symptoms of anxiety and depression.

Lisa also joined a support group for survivors of natural disasters, where she found comfort and validation from others who had gone through similar experiences. Through her therapy and support group, Lisa was able to create a new sense of meaning and purpose in life. She volunteered with disaster relief organizations and helped rebuild homes for others affected by the hurricane. Lisa also started a blog where she shared her experiences and encouraged others to seek help and support.

With time, Lisa was able to recover from the trauma of Hurricane Harvey and find joy in life again. She formed new friendships and felt a sense of community in the disaster relief organizations. Lisa also learned to appreciate the simple things in life and developed a sense of gratitude for what she had. Living Fully Beyond trauma helped Lisa find a new purpose in life and appreciate the value of helping others.

Lastly, finding meaning and purpose in life can be a powerful tool for long-term healing after trauma. Trauma can disrupt one's sense of purpose and meaning in life. However, finding meaning and purpose can help individuals find a sense of fulfillment and satisfaction in life. Some ways to find meaning and purpose in life after trauma include volunteering, engaging in hobbies, pursuing education or career goals, and helping others who have experienced similar trauma.

Living Fully Beyond trauma is a personal journey of healing and growth after a traumatic experience. The journey may involve therapy, support groups, hobbies, and community involvement. Successful Living Fully Beyond trauma experiences involve creating a new sense of meaning and purpose in life, forming healthy relationships with others, and finding joy and fulfillment in life. While the journey towards Living Fully Beyond trauma may be challenging, it is possible to heal and recover from trauma with the right support and resources. Though, long-term healing after trauma is a complex and ongoing process that requires a combination of therapeutic interventions, self-care practices, healthy relationships, a positive mindset, and finding meaning and purpose in life. Seeking professional help, engaging in self-care practices, building healthy relationships, cultivating a positive mindset, and finding meaning and purpose can all contribute to long-term healing after trauma. It is important to remember that healing is a unique and personal journey, and there is no one-size-fits-all approach. However, by taking small steps towards healing and being compassionate towards oneself, it is possible to live fully beyond trauma.

Notes:

Here is a sample 15-question survey to screen for the presence of trauma:

1. Have you ever experienced or witnessed a traumatic event, such as physical or sexual abuse, a natural disaster, a car accident, or combat?

2. Do you ever have unwanted, distressing memories or thoughts about the traumatic event?

3. Do you avoid reminders of the traumatic event, such as certain places or people?

4. Do you have trouble sleeping or have nightmares related to the traumatic event?

5. Do you feel jumpy, irritable, or easily startled?

6. Do you feel numb or detached from others and have difficulty experiencing emotions?

7. Do you feel guilty or responsible for the traumatic event, even if it was not your fault?

8. Have you ever experienced panic attacks or anxiety in response to reminders of the traumatic event?

9. Do you experience physical symptoms such as headaches or stomachaches that are not related to a medical condition?

10. Do you have difficulty trusting others or forming close relationships?

11. Have you ever turned to drugs, alcohol, or other substances to cope with the effects of the traumatic event?

12. Have you ever engaged in self-harming behaviors, such as cutting or burning, as a way to cope with the effects of the traumatic event?

13. Have you ever experienced suicidal thoughts or attempts as a result of the traumatic event?

14. Do you feel like the traumatic event has had a negative impact on your life in the long-term?

15. Have you ever sought help from a mental health professional to deal with the effects of the traumatic event?

It's important to note that a screening survey is not a diagnostic tool and should not be used to diagnose trauma or any other mental health condition. If someone scores high on this survey, it may indicate the need for further evaluation by a mental health professional.

Here are the 5 top phone numbers for those experiencing trauma in the United States:

1. National Suicide Prevention Lifeline: 1-800-273-TALK (8255) - Provides free, confidential support 24/7 for people in suicidal crisis or emotional distress.

2. National Domestic Violence Hotline: 1-800-799-SAFE (7233) - Offers crisis intervention, safety planning, and resources for survivors of domestic violence and their loved ones.

3. Substance Abuse and Mental Health Services Administration (SAMHSA) National Helpline: 1-800-662-HELP (4357) - Provides referrals to local treatment facilities, support groups, and counseling services for individuals and families facing mental health and substance abuse issues.

4. National Sexual Assault Hotline: 1-800-656-HOPE (4673) - Provides support and resources for survivors of sexual assault, as well as their friends and family.

5. Veterans Crisis Line: 1-800-273-8255, press 1 - Offers free, confidential support 24/7 for veterans and their families in crisis, including those experiencing trauma related to their military service.

It's important to note that these phone numbers are not a substitute for professional mental health treatment. Individuals experiencing trauma should seek treatment from a licensed mental health professional.

References:

Bonanno, G. A., & Mancini, A. D. (2012). The resilience factor: How coping with stress can strengthen us. Da Capo Press.

Keng, S. L., Smoski, M. J., & Robins, C. J. (2011). Effects of mindfulness on psychological health: A review of empirical studies. Clinical Psychology Review, 31(6), 1041-1056.

Neff, K. D. (2009). Self-compassion. In M. R. Leary & R. H. Hoyle (Eds.), Handbook of individual differences in social behavior (pp. 561-573). Guilford Press.

Norris, F. H., Tracy, M., & Galea, S. (2009). Looking for resilience: Understanding the longitudinal trajectories of responses to stress. Social Science & Medicine, 68(12), 2190-2198.

Enright, R. D., & Fitzgibbons, R. P. (2015). Forgiveness therapy: An empirical guide for resolving anger and restoring hope. American Psychological Association.

Fehr, R., Gelfand, M. J., & Nag, M. (2010). The road to forgiveness: A meta-analytic synthesis of its situational and dispositional correlates. Psychological bulletin, 136(5), 894.

Fredrickson, B. L. (2001). The role of positive emotions in positive psychology: The broaden-and-build theory of positive emotions. American psychologist, 56(3), 218.

Harris, A. H., Thoresen, C. E., & Lopez, S. J. (2007). Integrating positive psychology into counseling: Why and (when appropriate) how. Journal of counseling & development, 85(1), 3-13.

Lambert, N. M., Graham, S. M., Fincham, F. D., & Stillman, T. F. (2009). A changed perspective: How gratitude can affect sense of coherence through positive reframing. The Journal of Positive Psychology, 4(6), 461-470.

Luskin, F. (2002). Forgiveness: Heal your past and find the peace you deserve. HarperCollins.

McCullough, M. E., Fincham, F. D., & Tsang, J. (2003). Forgiveness, forbearance, and time: The temporal unfolding of transgression-related interpersonal motivations. Journal of personality and social psychology, 84(3), 540.

Neff, K. D., & Germer, C. K. (2013). A pilot study and randomized controlled trial of the mindful self-compassion program. Journal of Clinical Psychology, 69(1), 28-44.

Reed, G. L., & Enright, R. D. (2006). The effects of forgiveness therapy on depression, anxiety, and posttraumatic stress for women after spousal emotional abuse. Journal of consulting and clinical psychology, 74(5), 920.

Toussaint, L. L., Worthington Jr, E. L., & Williams, D. R. (2015). Forgiveness and health: scientific evidence and theories relating forgiveness to better health. Springer.

Bonanno, G. A., & Diminich, E. D. (2013). Annual research review: Positive adjustment to adversity–Trajectories of minimal-impact resilience and emergent resilience. Journal of Child Psychology and Psychiatry, 54(4), 378-401.

Foa, E. B., Hembree, E. A., & Rothbaum, B. O. (2007). Prolonged exposure therapy for PTSD: Emotional processing of traumatic experiences therapist guide. Oxford University Press.

Resick, P. A., Monson, C. M., & Chard, K. M. (2016). Cognitive processing therapy for PTSD: A comprehensive manual. Guilford Publications.

Tedeschi, R. G., & Calhoun, L. G. (2004). Posttraumatic growth: Conceptual foundations and empirical evidence. Psychological Inquiry, 15(1), 1-18.

Ullman, S. E., Townsend, S. M., Filipas, H. H., Starzynski, L. L., & Gallinari, C. (2007). Structural models of the relations of assault severity, social support, avoidance coping, self-blame, and PTSD among sexual assault survivors. Psychology of Women Quarterly, 31(1), 23-37.

American Psychiatric Association. (2013). Diagnostic and statistical manual of mental disorders (5th ed.). https://doi.org/10.1176/appi.books.9780890425596

Kolk, B. A., van der Hart, O., & Marmar, C. R. (2016). Dissociation and somatization in PTSD: Clinical and neurobiological perspectives. In R. A. Lanius, E. Vermetten, & C. Pain (Eds.), The hidden epidemic: The impact of early life trauma on health and disease (pp. 139-157). Cambridge University Press. https://doi.org/10.1017/CBO9781316273890.009

National Institute of Mental Health. (2018, July). Post-traumatic stress disorder. https://www.nimh.nih.gov/health/topics/post-traumatic-stress-disorder-ptsd/index.shtml

Neff, K. D. (2011). Self-compassion, self-esteem, and well-being. Social and Personality Psychology Compass, 5(1), 1-12.

Shakespeare-Finch, J., & Lurie-Beck, J. (2014). A meta-analytic clarification of the relationship between posttraumatic growth and symptoms of posttraumatic distress disorder. Journal of Anxiety Disorders, 28(3), 223-229.

Ullman, S. E. (2010). Social support and recovery from sexual assault: A review. Aggression and Violent Behavior, 15(1), 1-13.

Calhoun, L. G., & Tedeschi, R. G. (2006). The foundations of posttraumatic growth: An expanded framework. In L. G. Calhoun & R. G. Tedeschi (Eds.), Handbook of posttraumatic growth: Research and practice (pp. 3-23). Psychology Press.

Park, C. L. (2010). Making sense of the meaning literature: An integrative review of meaning making and its effects on adjustment to stressful life events. Psychological Bulletin, 136(2), 257-301

Cook, J. M., Dinnen, S., Simiola, V., Bernardy, N., Rosenheck, R., & Hoff, R. (2014). Influence of exposure to combat and operational deployment on mental health symptoms and disorders in female veterans. Journal of Women's Health, 23(10), 781-788.

Dohrenwend, B. P., Turner, J. B., Turse, N. A., Lewis-Fernández, R., & Yager, T. J. (2016). War-related posttraumatic stress disorder in Black, Hispanic, and majority White Vietnam War veterans: The roles of exposure and vulnerability. Journal of Traumatic Stress, 29(5), 462-470.

Khoury, N. M., Lutz, J., & Mekawi, Y. (2018). Trauma-focused cognitive behavioral therapy: A review of the evidence base. Trauma, Violence, & Abuse, 19(2), 227-248.

Rosenberg, L., Prener, C. G., Gargano, L. M., & Williams, M. (2017). Promoting resilience and recovery in the aftermath of disasters and traumatic events. American Journal of Public Health, 107(S2), S133-S136.

Scherrer, J. F., Salas, J., Lustman, P. J., Hauptman, P. J., & Chrusciel, T. (2015). PTSD is associated with an increased risk of hypertension. Journal of Anxiety Disorders, 32, 83-88.

Van der Kolk, B. A. (2015). The body keeps the score: Brain, mind, and body in the healing of trauma. Penguin Books.

Weathers, F. W., Litz, B. T., Keane, T. M., Palmieri, P. A., Marx, B. P., & Schnurr, P. P. (2013). The PTSD checklist for DSM-5 (PCL-5). Scale available from the National Center for PTSD at www.ptsd.va.gov.

Saxe, G. N., Ellis, B. H., Fogler, J., & Hansen, S. (2005). Somatic complaints among sexually abused children. Journal of the American Academy of Child & Adolescent Psychiatry, 44(10), 1085-1092.

Watkins, L. E., Sprang, G., & Rothbaum, B. O. (2011). Treating PTSD in military personnel: A clinical review. Journal of the American Medical Association, 306(5), 549-557.

Monson, C. M., Schnurr, P. P., Resick, P. A., Friedman, M. J., Young-Xu, Y., & Stevens, S. P. (2006). Cognitive processing therapy for veterans with military-related posttraumatic stress disorder. Journal of Consulting and Clinical Psychology, 74(5), 898-907.

Norris, F. H., Friedman, M. J., Watson, P. J., Byrne, C. M., Diaz, E., & Kaniasty, K. (2009). 60,000 disaster victims speak: Part I. An empirical review of the empirical literature, 1981-2001. Psychiatry: Interpersonal and Biological Processes, 72(3), 217-239.

Larkin, K. T., Choi, K., & McKee, L. G. (2016). Mindfulness-based interventions for PTSD: A systematic review and meta-analysis. International Journal of Behavioral Medicine, 23(2), 227-246.

Herman, J. L. (1992). Complex PTSD: A syndrome in survivors of prolonged and repeated trauma. Journal of traumatic stress, 5(3), 377-391.

EST:2009